ACPL ITEM
DISCARDED

SO-CHH-423

WHAT ON EARTH

by Robert O. Bale

Published by the American Camping Association
Bradford Woods
Martinsville, Indiana 46151

SEP 1 '69

Copyright © 1969 by American Camping Association, Inc.
Bradford Woods
Martinsville, Indiana 46151

Cover photo courtesy of
Camp Nebagamon
Lake Nebagamon, Wisconsin

Price of $3.95

Standard Book Number 87603-000-2
Library of Congress catalog card number: 74-84605
All rights reserved.
Printed in the United States of America

1518102

IN TRIBUTE TO
MARY GWYNN 1894-1967

Mary Gwynn had a rare sense of the beauty and wonder in nature and was able to awaken in children an awareness and appreciation of the world about them. She chose Gay Valley for her camp because of its infinite natural beauty and what living there might mean to children.

Her quiet influence continues to have great impact on camping. In tribute, her many friends have made possible, through the Fund For Advancement of Camping, the continuation of her Nature Institute in the American Camping Association's Southeastern Section as well as this book.

Eleanor P. Eells
Fund for Advancement
of Camping

*Dedicated
to my daughter
Patti*

From our most distant ancestors we have inherited an instinct that leads us to do, in the name of recreation, the things that they did for survival. The things that we do for fun, they did of necessity. They hunted and fished for food enough to stay alive. We do them for fun. They learned to make and use a bow and arrow, a boomerang, or a spear to procure food and to protect themselves. Archery and other field sports, such as javelin throwing, are a part of modern recreation. Living in a crude shelter and cooking over an open fire helped them to stay alive. We go camping, cook our meals over a campfire, or barbecue steaks in our backyards. We certainly do not need these things to survive so why do we do them? It must be because of inherited instincts that lead us to do the same types of things as our ancient ancestors.

To add greater satisfaction to our periods of recreation, we need to know how and why our ancestors developed their skills; how they fitted into their environments in those early days; and how we can do similar things to enhance our own lives.

This book is intended to provide a background of knowledge concerning the earth and its resources including mankind, useful in planning and carrying out successful programs of youth activities. From material found herein, a leader of young people can provide a full program of interesting and valuable outdoor activity.

—Robert O. Bale

CONTENTS

Part 1

FROM THE BEGINNING

WONDERS AND MYSTERIES OF THE EARTH

We know that the earth is a huge ball, spinning on its axis, and rushing through space.

If we could weigh the earth, measuring it in tons, we would come up with a figure of about 6 sextillion, 570 quintillion tons. That would be written like this - 6,570,000,000,000,000,-000,000 tons.

On the outside of the earth there are from a few inches to a few feet of topsoil over layers of solid rock 30 - 50 miles in thickness. In depressions on the surface are lakes, seas, and oceans.

Below the many layers of solid rock is a very dense hot rock, hot enough to melt, but probably not melted because of the immense pressure of about 150,000 pounds per square inch which holds it rigid. This dense rock, called the "outer mantle" is about 600 miles thick.

Beneath the outer mantle is another layer about 1200 miles thick through which earthquake shocks travel as though it were made of steel. It is probably made up of iron and other metals and is called the "intermediate layer."

Below this intermediate layer is the earth's core under a tremendous pressure of about 45 million pounds per square inch. It is believed to be composed of iron and nickel.

We have learned that the earth is spherical and moves in two principal ways. These two motions of the earth which affect our daily lives are its rotation on its axis once each day and its revolving around the sun once each year. Rotation gives us day and night, and the revolution around the sun gives us our year with its four seasons. One revolution around the sun provides us with our measurement of the length of life and of the march through time of the events of history.

How the Earth May Have Been Formed

Since the earth and all of the other planets revolve in the same direction and their orbits are nearly circular, it is theo-

WHAT ON EARTH

rized that the solar system condensed from a whirling cloud of gas called a "nebula" which, as it cooled and condensed, left successive rings of matter which eventually condensed into the planets. The sun is the hot, remaining center of the original nebula.

Another theory holds that long ago, a great star, passing close to the sun, attracted streams of matter from the sun by its gravitational pull, and set them whirling. These later condensed forming the planets.

The Age of the Earth

Radioactive tests show the earth to be more than three billion years old. Since the crust must have been solid for these tests on ancient rock to be effective, the earth must have been a hot, whirling body at least five billion years ago.

The Face of the Earth Changes

The face of the earth is constantly changing. Some parts are moving upwards to form mountains; others are steadily sinking. Most important of the changes to us are the changes made by water which is constantly at work wearing down the higher lands and building up the lowlands by filling in ponds, lakes, and oceans. Almost ¾ of the earth's surface is covered by water. Most of this is in oceans of salt water resulting from millions of years of water dissolving salts from the earth's crust and carrying them to the oceans where they have remained. Man and most animals and plants cannot use salt water so they must depend upon evaporation of water from the oceans, returning to the earth again as rain.

Measuring Time on Earth

The largest divisions of geologic time are called "eras." Each era began with probable great world-wide changes in the earth's crust when new mountains were formed causing physical conditions on earth to change radically. The name of each era reflects the development and changes of life on earth caused by these physical changes in the earth itself.

Each era's name usually ends in "zoic" from the Greek word "zoe" meaning "life." The earliest eras are called the Cosmic and Azoic Eras; Cosmic when the first primordial materials were assembling to form the earth and Azoic when the earth became solidified.

The latest, or Cenozoic Era, is probably just at its beginning and, although it is estimated to be 70 million years old already, it is supposedly still in its first period. The subdivisions also reflect the development of life. These are the "epochs" (subdivisions of a period). Their names also reflect the proportion of known plants and animals that were in existence during the epoch.

How Life Began

Biologists theorize that the first forms of life came from the gathering of chemical elements to form compounds similar to a virus. Through the ages these became living cells which eventually gave rise to plants and animals. The oldest fossils showing individual cells are those of algae about 1.8 billion years old. Within the next 1,200,000,000 years, these had developed from the single-cell algae to huge dinosaurs, and life on our planet was well under way. Possible evidence of man goes back only a few thousand years so he is only a most recent addition to our planet. Is it not possible that within the next few million years man, like the dinosaurs, may also become extinct with some much higher form of life dominant?

North American Submerges

It was during the Ordivician Period of the Paleozoic Era that North America was almost completely submerged beneath the seas. Only the coastal mountain ranges plus parts of Canada and a few islands remained above water. The islands were located in the Adirondacks, the Ozarks, Wisconsin, Ohio, and Kentucky. Evidence of this submergence is found in many marine fossils. This period also resulted in the oil deposits which are now being exploited in many parts of the country. The marble of Vermont and Tennessee is also a result.

The huge salt deposits of New York State came during the Silurian Period which followed. Great seas evaporated, leaving their salt in thick beds extending over much of the Northeast from New York to Michigan and south as far as Tennessee.

North America Rises Again

Modern life in North America began in the Cretaceous Period of the Mesozoic Era, perhaps 100 million years ago when the ancestors of the Rocky Mountains were formed. As the land rose, great swamps were drained and the lush swamp growth which had provided food for the great plant-eating dinosaurs disappeared, leading to the end of the Age of Reptiles and leaving the earth ready for the development of mammals.

THE EARTH'S TIMETABLE

The timetable of the development of life on earth is divided into Eras and Periods, each of which had its own dominant form of life or the beginnings of life. Each Period is divided into Epochs.

Cosmic and Azoic Eras - more than 3 billion years ago. During the Azoic Era the earth became solid with oceans and atmosphere but no life.

Archeozoic Era - began more than 2 billion years ago. There are no fossils left from this Era. Life was composed of single cells probably living in the seas. This era is sometimes called the time of the virus-like beginnings of life.

Proterozoic Era - began about 1.7 billion years ago. A few fossil algae remain from this era. Life was composed of simple marine invertebrates and algae.

Paleozoic Era - began about 540 million years ago and lasted for some 335 million years. It includes the following Periods:

Cambrian Period
Ordovician Period
Silurian Period
Devonian Period
Mississippian Period
Pennsylvanian Period
Permian Period

Many fossils remain from this era. Life included invertebrates having shells, trilobites, starfish, primitive sharks, lungfish, amphibians, spore-bearing plants, and forests.

Pelycosaur (Paleozoic Era)

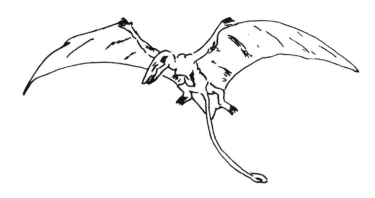

Pterodactyl (Mesozoic Era)

Mesozoic Era -	began about 200 million years ago.

Triassic Period
Jurassic Period
Cretaceous Period

This is called the "Age of Reptiles" with dinosaurs appearing as well as pterodactyls, brontosaurs and stagosaurs. There were egg-laying mammals and birds with teeth (archeopteryx). Towards the end of this era, the dinosaurs became extinct and flowering plants and modern insects first appeared.

Cenozoic Era - 70 million years ago.

Paleocene Period
Eocene Period
Oligocene Period
Miocene Period
Pleistocene Period
Halocene (Recent) Period

From the Beginning

This is called the "Age of Mammals." Early in this era, the first primitive monkeys, horses, and elephants appeared. The earliest mammals became extinct and finally man appeared and became dominant. The Halocene or Recent Period began about 25,000 years ago.

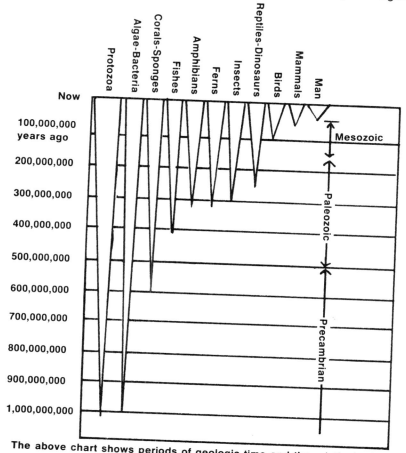

The above chart shows periods of geologic time and the relatively short amount of time that man has been on earth.

DOMINANT FORMS OF LIFE

All living things are divided into two kingdoms called the Plant Kingdom and the Animal Kingdom.

Plant Kingdom - Within the Plant Kingdom there are four groupings ranging from the simplest plants to the most complex seed-bearing plants. These groupings are called "Phylum" and are designated as follows:

Thallophyta - These are the simplest plants having no true roots, stems, or leaves. They include the algae having chlorophyl, kelp, seawee, fungi having no chlorophyl, bacteria, molds, mushrooms, and yeast.

Bryophyta - These are the mosses and liverworts which have simple leaves but without true roots and stems. They reproduce by spores.

Pteridophyta - This phylum has true roots, stems and leaves. The plants are spore-bearing and include ferns, club mosses, and horsetails.

Spermatophyta - Here are the plants with true roots, stems, leaves, and seeds. There are the Gymnosperms such as the pines and hemlocks having naked seeds; the Angiosperms which have flowering seeds; the Monocots such as corn, grains, lilies, etc.; and the Dicots such as beans, nuts and apples.

Animal Kingdom - There are ten Phylum in the Animal Kingdom starting with single-celled animals and ending with mammals as we know them.

Protozoa - These are single-celled animals some of which live on other animals as parasites. They reproduce both sexually and asexually and include the amoeba, paramecium, etc.

Porifera - These animals have two cell layers having a flexible or rigid skeleton. They reproduce both sexually and asexually and include the sponges.

Coelenterata - These are characterized by being hollow-bodied. They have two cell layers and carry tentacles with stinging cells. Among these are the coral, hydra and jellyfish.

Platyhelminthes - These are the flat worms having three-cell-layered bodies. Most of them are parasitic. They include the tapeworm, liver flukes, and plenaria.

Nemethelminthes - Here are the round worms with long unsegmented bodies. They have a variety of organ systems and are mostly parasitic. Here are found the hookworms and trichina.

Annelida - These are the segmented worms having simple circulatory and nervous systems. These include the earthworm, leech, and sandworm.

Echinodermata - They are the spinyskinned marine animals having complex organs and true nerves. Included are the starfish, sand dollar, sea urchin, and sea lily.

Mollusca - These clams, oysters, snails, octopus, and squid are softbodied and unsegmented.

Arthropoda - These are segmented and have exterior skeletons. They have jointed feet and well developed nervous systems. They include the spider, lobster, centipedes, and insects.

Chordata - This Phylum includes the true Vertebrates as follows:

fish - These are cold blooded, have gills, air bladders,

scales, a chambered heart and lay eggs having a gelatinous covering.

amphibians - These are cold-blooded and develop lungs as they reach maturity. They have a 3-chambered heart and naked skins. Their eggs have a gelatinous covering. Among them are the frogs and toads.

reptiles - They breath into lungs at birth; are cold-blooded; have 3-chambered hearts; and lay eggs covered with a membrane. Included are snakes and lizards.

birds - These are warm-blooded and have lungs with many air-sacs. They have feathers, hollow bones, wings, scales on legs and a 4-chambered heart. Their eggs are covered with shells made of lime.

mammals - They are warm-blooded having 4-chambered hearts. They are also characterized by hair, a diaphragm, seven neck bones and lungs having many air sacs. They have mammary glands and most young are born alive. This group includes man.

THE GREAT LIZARDS

The word "dinosaur" comes from the Greek and may be literally translated to mean "great lizard". Actually the dinosaurs were not lizards but may have been the ancestors of our crocodiles. It has been only during the last century and a half that mankind has had the knowledge that such things as dinosaurs existed. It is thought that dinosaurs became extinct long before mankind came into being.

The first discoveries of the remains of dinosaurs were made in England. The discoverers tried to identify them as parts of familiar animals. It was not until 1842 that Sir Richard Owen gave the name of "dinosaur" to these animals that had been forgotten on earth but still remained as giant fossils.

Beginning about 180 million years ago, dinosaurs became the largest land animals that have ever lived on earth. They existed for about 105 million years but as their environment changed they could not survive and about 75 million years ago they became extinct.

Dinosaurs came in all sizes from the giant brontosaurus, stegosaurus and megalosaurus to tiny dinosaurs no larger than wild turkey. Some were plant-eaters and others flesh-eaters, but man and dinosaurs never ate each other for they lived some millions of years apart.

THE BEGINNING OF MANKIND

We know little about the oldest and most primitive man, the Java Man. In 1891 on the island of Java the top of a skull, three teeth, and a thighbone, all that remained of the skeleton of an ancient man, were discovered. From these few pieces, scientists reconstructed a complete skull, very thick but with a very small brain. The remains of Peking Man (nearly as old as the Java Man) found in China indicate a larger brain. Both had large jaws and teeth, probably used for fighting. As man progressed, his jaws and teeth became smaller and his brain larger. Peking Man had already advanced to the point where he had learned to use fire, to hunt, and to make and use crude tools. The Neanderthal Man lived for approximately 100,000 years until about 50,000 years ago when the Cro-Magnon Man had developed with a brain even larger than the average man's brain of today. He learned to think, to make plans, and even how to express himself through painting.

The present race of man began some 20,000 to 25,000 years ago and soon developed more skills. At first he had few skills of any kind; no tools or weapons; no language; no clothing or shelter; no knowledge of how to build a fire or cook food. His first tool was probably a stick which became a club or spear when needed; or it may have been a stone which fitted his hand well, and which in need was used as a weapon or a hammer. Perhaps in cracking a nut, or in pounding one stone against another, a stone broke leaving a sharp edge that would cut. These were the first beginnings of modern tools.

Man's first knowledge of fire was certainly from fires caused by lightning or volcanic eruptions. At first fire was his enemy. It probably took man a few thousand years to find that he could keep a fire going and control it, and still more thousands of years to learn how to start a fire by striking sparks from flint or by friction. He had to learn the value of controlled fire and its uses before he desired fire for warmth and cooking. It must be remembered that no animal except man has ever learned to make fire. This was one of his greatest steps towards civilization.

How did he learn to cook? We suppose that he may have smelled the agreeable odor of wild game killed and cooked by a forest fire, started perhaps by lightning, or he may have accidently dropped a piece of meat in the fire while warming himself as he was eating his raw meat.

He certainly learned the value of clothing during the ice age, or to protect himself from his environment.

With his knowledge of fire, cooking, making and using tools with sharp edges, and clothing, man was well on his way towards dominance of the earth. His progress for the first several thousand years was slow, however, and his real progress is very recent. In fact mankind has progressed farther in the last 50 years than in the many thousands of years of both recorded and unrecorded history before that time. This will most certainly be true of the next 50 years as well.

FOSSILS

The Study of Paleontology

Scientists have pieced together many strange relationships through the study of fossils. The sheep, camel, giraffe, hippoptamus, and moose are thought to have developed from a single kind of primitive ancestor. Both the horse and rhinocerus are thought to have come from the tiny "eohippus," no larger than a small dog.

The farther our study of fossils goes back into time, the smaller we find that the brain-space of animals was as compared to their size. The great reptiles, such as the dinosaurs, reached a length of as much as 100 feet but had very small brains in relation to their size. These huge animals became extinct, leaving creatures smaller in size, but having larger brains.

From the Paleozoic Era there are many fossil remains of early life on earth still to be found, dating back as far as 540 million years ago. These include the trilobites, starfish, many shellfish, early amphibians and spore-bearing plants and trees.

The age of reptiles began about 200 million years ago in the Mesozoic Era and the fossil remains of many of the dinosaurs, flowers, and insects of this era may be found.

The word "fossil" comes from a Latin word meaning "to dig," but we do not always have to dig to find fossils. Many of these are found on the surface of the soil or along stream banks where water erosion has uncovered them. We may come across them in our stone sidewalks and in the building stone used in our homes and business places.

Through the study of fossils, scientists can piece together the history of life on earth. Through fossils we know that the Rocky Mountains and even the Alps were once below the surface of the ocean for the fossils of sea animals are found on their slopes. From fossil remains, we know that early camels once roamed North America; that many plants once grew in the polar regions and that tropical forests once covered the United States.

Limestone, used in many of today's buildings, is composed of the shells of tiny animals that lived in the seas millions of years ago.

Fossils are found in many forms. They may be the imprints of leaves or ferns or the tracks of a prehistoric dinosaur made in mud which later hardened into rock. Sometimes we find the actual bones and teeth of ancient animals preserved in dry areas. Other fossils are in the form of minerals that have replaced an animal, plant, or tree buried in ancient mud or silt. In some cases even the flesh of ancient animals has been found frozen in ice formed thousands of years ago.

Early Man

The latest of all fossil remains include the fossils of early man, usually dating back less than 25,000 years. They have been discovered with the remains of the mammoth and cave bear which early man killed for food.

Man, with a greater brain space in relation to his body size, soon became dominant on earth. Think of the remarkable development of man during the past 25,000 years in relation to the development of animals over many millions of years. As far as we know, man is the only animal which has developed the ability to reason and to plan and, through reading and writing, to make use of the experience of other men.

Where Fossils Are Found

Fossils are found almost everywhere on earth. In the United States, well-known deposits of the fossils of the great reptiles and mammals, include those of Nebraska, Colorado, South Dakota, California, and Wyoming. The La Brea asphalt pits in California were a trap for prehistoric saber-toothed tigers, horses, mastodons, giant sloths, wolves, primitive camels, huge buffalos as well as thousands of lesser animals. Their remains have been remarkably well-preserved at this site.

Fossil algae have been found in polar regions in so great a concentration as to color the ice and snow.

Look for fossils in the shales of creek beds, in stone quarries and in places where water has cut deep stream beds. In the northeastern part of the United States we find the fossils of shellfish by the millions as well as the fossils of early animals, plants, and trees. Most abundant are the brachiopods (lamp shells) and crinoids (stems of sea lilies).

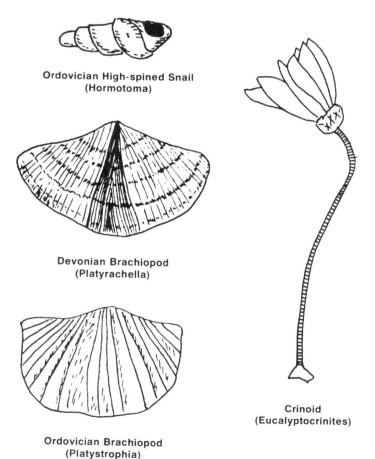

Ordovician High-spined Snail
(Hormotoma)

Devonian Brachiopod
(Platyrachella)

Ordovician Brachiopod
(Platystrophia)

Crinoid
(Eucalyptocrinites)

HUNTING FOR LITTLE CLIMATES

We have seen that climate affected the development of early plants, animals, insects, and man. We usually think of climate as the combination of weather factors for large areas of the earth. People are affected by the sum of weather conditions over large areas.

People are but a small part of nature, however. Trees, plants, insects, most animals, and some birds need little climates in a relatively small area. Climates for each of these refers only to the area in which they live. If we hunt for them, we can find many places where we find that temperature, humidity, air movement, radiation and precipitation vary from the general climate of the larger area and are actually little climates in themselves. Each of these little climates has its own residents that are generally not to be found over a larger climate area.

Where Are These Little Climates?

These little climates may be the opposite sides of a hill, near a waterfall or an asphalt road, by a spring or bog, in the woods, or on barren soil or rocks. The places where they may be found are endless.

How Do We Explore Them?

To explore these little climates, let's make use of a thermometer and a compass.

Select an area. Take temperature readings on the north, east, south, and west sides of trees, bushes, and buildings within the area. Record them on paper.

Record temperatures of the same spots at different times of the day. How do they vary? If there is water present, check and record the temperature at different depths. What is the temperature of the surface of the ground? How about 6 inches below the surface? A foot below?

What plants, trees, insects, birds, and animals are found there? Are they the same as you find in a different type of little climate?

Can Living Things Change These Climates?

In a small way they can be changed. A bird fluffs its feathers in cold weather, a man puts on warmer clothing, a woodchuck digs a hole. Each is creating a "little climate" close to his body where he can remain comfortable. Man builds a house, sets up a tent, erects an awning, or installs air-conditioning to control his own little climate.

In exploring little climates, a camp counselor should point out the relationships of all kinds of life to variations in climate. Mankinds' enjoyment in the out-of-doors is closely related to his understanding of little climates and of what prefers to live in each one.

Part 2

PIONEER'S NECESSITY

TODAY'S RECREATION

MAN BUILDS ON DISCOVERY

With the development of the ability to think, to remember, and to reason, mankind started his rise above the other animals. Speech developed from the first sounds that man made in an effort to communicate with other men. Many thousands of years later, man invented the alphabet and learned to use a written means of communication. His first discovery of great importance to the development of civilization was that he could start and control fire. Sometime, probably a few thousand years later, he discovered the principle of the wheel, first using round logs or stones for moving heavy objects, and then slowly developing a wooden wheel in the shape we know today.

We can go through all of the stages of the development of early mankind for ourselves, especially in a camp situation where we can learn the arts and crafts of early man. It is interesting that most of our sports and recreation of today are adaptations of skills that early man depended upon for survival. Our baseball bats date back to his club, our balls to the rocks that he threw to protect himself and his family or to obtain food, our guns to his bow and arrows, our javelin throwing to his spear, our competitive group games to his wars between tribes.

Let's start with fire and learn to make it and control it as he did.

MAN CONTROLS FIRE

Fire by Friction

Starting a fire by friction is probably the oldest fire-starting method known, and preceded the dawn of history by thousands of years. Although several methods of providing the necessary friction have been used throughout the world, the bow and drill method is the best known and is the easiest to make and use. The woods used should be soft enough to wear away but also hard enough so that plenty of heat is generated by the friction between the drill and the fireboard.

The best woods to use in making a fire-by-friction kit are these: balsa (particularly good for the drill), red cedar, white cedar, basswood, larch, white pine, sycamore, poplar, yucca, willow, and soft maple.

To be certain that the wood is acceptable for fire-making, try this test: If, when using the drill, the dust that comes from the fireboard is brown and coarse, the wood is too soft. If the dust is very fine and there is not much of it, the wood is too hard.

Needed to produce fire are these things—

A bow, 2-2½ feet in length. This may be made from a piece of springy seasoned wood, such as ash or hickory, or it may be a green branch that is stiff but springy.

A bow string of rawhide leather. This may be a bootlace purchased from a shoe store.

A drill made from well-seasoned wood of one of the varieties listed.

A drill socket to be placed on top of the drill to hold it in place while it is being twirled.

Tinder to catch the fire.

WHAT ON EARTH

A fire pan — a chip or small board to catch the wood dust and the spark produced by friction.

A fire-board — ½ to ¾ inch thick and of any convenient length and width to be carried easily. Preferably, it should be of the same kind of wood as the drill.

Constructing The Device:

Making the bow —

Cut shallow notches about 1 inch from each end of the bow, or cut a notch at one end and drill a small hole at the other. Tie the thong around the notches, or thread it through the hole at one end of the bow, tying a knot, so it will not slide through, and wrapping around the notch at the other end. The thong should be loose enough to wrap once around the drill but should have enough tension to bend the bow slightly and to prevent slipping on the drill while being used.

Making the drill —

The drill is about one foot in length. Trim it to a blunt point at the lower end and a somewhat sharper point at the top end. This is the end to be held with the drill socket and should provide for as little friction as possible. Trim the center part of the drill to a more or less six-sided shape to help keep the thong from slipping.

Making the drill socket —

Using a piece of hardwood about 2 inches square, make a small hollow in the center with a jackknife or drill and sand the hollow smooth. Shape the outside of the socket to fit the hand. The socket is to be held on the top of the drill while it is being twirled and is used to create pressure on the drill.

Making the fireboard —

Make this about 12 inches long and 4 inches wide. At one inch intervals, cut or drill hollows in the top of the fireboard about one inch from the edge. With a jackknife or saw, cut V-shaped notches from the edge of the fireboard to the center of each hole, making the V wider at the bottom than at the top. The hollows on the top of the fireboard are to hold the working end of the drill as the drilling is begun.

Making the tinder —

Use one of the following: the finely shredded outer bark of red or white cedar or of yellow (grey) birch, or the shredded inner bark of cottonwood, chestnut or slippery elm. The dry fine material from a mouse nest or flying squirrel nest is excellent.

To shred, scrape the bark with a knife or piece of glass, or pound it between two sticks or stones. Dry it thoroughly before using.

Starting the fire:

The fireboard is placed on the ground with the fire pan or chip beneath the notch being used. Directly under the notch and over the fireboard, place a small amount of tinder.

Pass the leather thong of the bow once around the drill in such a manner that the drill is on the outer side of the thong away from the bow. The thong should be taut enough so that there is a slight bend in the bow.

The bottom (blunt) end of the drill is placed in the small pit above the notch in the fireboard and the left foot is placed on the fireboard to hold it securely. Kneel with the left arm against the outside of the left leg. The socket is held in the left hand and placed over the top end of the drill.

WHAT ON EARTH

Draw the bow back and forth with long, steady strokes keeping pressure with the socket on the top of the drill and increasing the pressure slightly with each stroke of the bow. Friction between the drill and the fireboard will cause the drill to bore into the wood at the notch. Wood dust will fall through the notch onto the tinder and fire pan beneath the notch. At first this dust will be brown, but will soon become black and start to smoke. As soon as smoke appears steadily from the wood dust and tinder on the fire pan, blow it gently until a glowing coal is seen. Continue blowing and add tinder until it becomes a blaze.

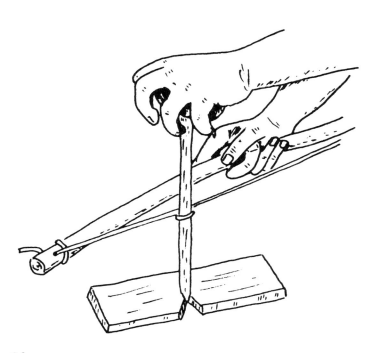

Add more tinder, then fine kindling and the fire will soon be going well.

Practice until you become proficient and then teach others to start a fire by friction.

Fire with Flint and Steel   1518102

Starting your own fire using either the friction method or with flint and steel can add a great amount of satisfaction to a campout or cookout. Using flint and steel is not too difficult and was one of the ways of fire-starting used by thousands of people before the invention of the match.

Needed to start a fire by this method are:

A fair-sized piece of flint which you may be able to find in a stream bed or which may be a broken arrow head.

A piece of hardened steel, preferably a 4-5 inch piece of an old file although any good steel will do, even the back of a jackknife.

A piece of charred cotton rope or cotton cloth.

Tinder such as described in the previous article on *Fire by Friction.*

A small tin box such as shoe polish, salve, small nails, etc. may have come in.

A small bag to carry your fire-making kit.

Charring Cotton Rope or Cloth:

Use small pieces of cotton rope or strips of cotton cloth or flannel. Char by holding them over the tin container and setting them afire, one at a time. When they are blazing well, drop them into the tin and cover tightly to smother the flame. When several strips have been charred, they may be carried in the same container as a part of your fire-starting kit.

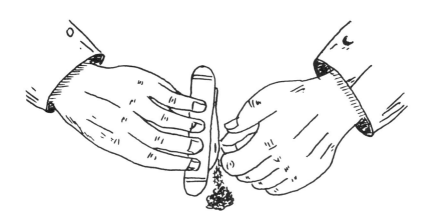

Starting the Fire:

To start the fire, wrap the flint in the charred cloth, leaving a corner of the flint exposed. Strike the steel downward against the exposed point of flint to make sparks fly into the charred cloth. As the cloth starts to smolder, blow on it gently until it flames. Place the flaming cloth in some of the tinder and as it burns add larger, dry pieces of kindling wood that you have gathered in advance.

MAN MAPS HIS TRAVELS

The Story of Map-Making

Primitive man knew the world only as far as he could see it on his short travels. These were only to reach a better hunting ground, to obtain water and salt, to escape his enemies, or to find a better and safer place in which to live. Crude drawings of his routes, along with the animals he saw, have been found on the walls of the caves in which he lived and have been recognized as the earliest form of maps. As he became more traveled, the importance of his maps grew, covering greater areas and showing landmarks in greater detail.

The oldest map known to have been made by civilized man is in the form of a small clay tablet from Babylonia, made more than 2000 years ago.

Early maps were mostly guesswork for there were many unknowns such as the shapes and sizes of land masses and bodies of water. It took thousands of years for map-making to develop into the science we know today.

We do not know who invented the compass but until its invention it was almost impossible to describe directions, particularly at sea. The first attempts at giving direction were in relation to the prevailing winds, the dawns, and sunsets, towards the oceans or the mountains or towards the moon and stars. Some of these were constantly changing as the earth turned on its axis and rotated around the sun, or as the seasons changed.

Ptolemy a scientist of the Second Century, devised two ways to help in producing more accurate maps. These were the astrolabe used to measure the angles of known stars, and an instrument used to measure the height of the shadow cast by the sun, and from this, to find the latitude of a place.

Present day map-makers make use of many new devices unknown to ancient man. Photography, triangulation, satellites, radar, and electronic devices are all in use.

WHAT ON EARTH

For space travel we are once more endeavoring to find better ways of describing direction for in space there is no north, south, east, or west.

The Development of Map and Compass

It is doubtful if man ever had the ability to migrate as birds do, using instinct to guide them from one place to another and back again. Early man simply wandered using the land-marks he could remember to get back to his home again.

Before he learned to communicate by writing, he learned to draw and paint. His first maps were the pictures which he drew to tell others where he had been and what he had seen. Even today we find many of our maps using pictured objects to show what may be found in certain areas.

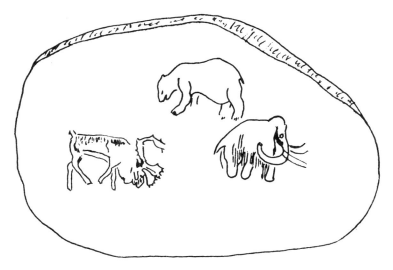

Crude drawings on cave walls have been recognized as being the earliest forms of maps.

Since the very earliest times, men have found directions from the North Star and the moon and sun. These are not the best direction givers, however, for they are constantly changing their places and are often covered by clouds. Sometime, well before the 12th century, man found that nature had provided an accurate means to determine north and south in the form of a magnetized iron called lodestone. When a piece of magnetized iron is placed on a wood chip floating in water, the wood will swing its position until the magnetized iron is pointing north and south. It was a magnetic compass that helped Magellan and Columbus make their historic voyages. Present day compasses make use of a magnetized needle and present day maps are drawn using accurate directions determined by a compass during the drawing process.

WHAT ON EARTH

The compass works because of its relationship to the earth which happens to be a huge magnet. The earth's magnetic poles are not exactly the same as the geographic poles. Connecting the two magnetic poles are "lines of force" and the compass needle aligns itself with these "lines of force" in the earth's magnetic field. Where the "lines of force" happen to lie along a meridian, the compass will point to true north. Elsewhere it points either to the east or west of true north. This difference from true north is known as "declination" and is used in making and reading maps.

There are certain plants, known as compass plants, which have leaves that point north and south. This is caused by intense sunlight and dry air which causes these plants to turn their leaves edgewise to escape the heat of the sun. To obtain what light they need, their leaves turn their flat surfaces to the morning and evening rays of the sun consequently pointing north and south. Among these plants are the prickly lettuce and rosinweeds found in America and the eucalyptus of Australia.

The Pioneer Makes His Own Compass

America was explored and settled by men who had great skill in finding their way by day and night, through forests and mountains, and across great lakes and prairies without a compass or map to tell them where they were going or in what direction.

They were adept at using their own senses and the signs found in nature to tell them the right direction.

They learned to follow a straight line by sighting two landmarks ahead of them and when they reached the first, again sighting ahead in a straight line. They could never go in a circle by this method.

They also learned a number of methods of determining north and south, east and west. From these they could easily determine other compass directions.

Stake and Shadow Method (Sunny day)

Sometime during the forenoon, drive a 3-4 ft. stake into the ground. At the end of the shadow cast by the stake, drive a wooden peg.

Now, using a cord, tie one end loosely around the bottom of the stake. Using the distance of the stake from the peg as a radius, scratch an arc of a circle on the ground so that as the shadow of the stake moves, it follows the direction of the arc.

At the moment in the afternoon when the shadow again just touches the scratched arc, drive another peg at this point. Now scratch another line between the two pegs which you have driven into the ground. This line will run east and west with the end of the morning shadow being west.

Another line scratched perpendicular to this line and touching the bottom of the stake will be a north-south line with the bottom of the stake being the south end.

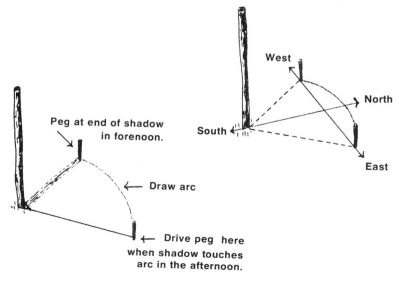

Peg at end of shadow in forenoon.

West

North

South

East

← Draw arc

← Drive peg here when shadow touches arc in the afternoon.

WHAT ON EARTH

Shadow-top Method (Sunny day)

Drive a 3-4 ft. stake into the ground in a vertical position. Drive a peg into the ground where the top of the stake's shadow falls. About one half hour later, drive a second peg where the top of the shadow falls at this time.

A straight line drawn between these two pegs will be very close to a true east-west line. The first peg will always be the west end of the line.

Shadowless Method (Sunny day)

Using a 2-3 ft. stake, drive it into the ground in such a position that the top of the stake points directly towards the sun and the stake casts no shadow.

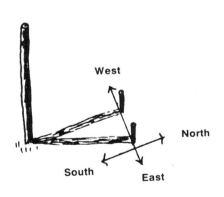

Now wait until the stake does cast a shadow at least six inches long. This shadow will extend in an east-west direction with west being towards the base of the stake. On the first day of spring and the first day of autumn, the

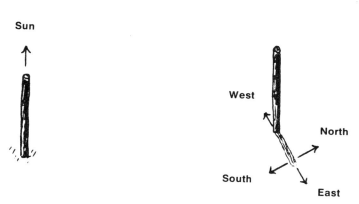

Sun

West

North

South

East

shadow will be on a true east-west line. The greatest variation will be on the longest day of the year (in June) and the shortest day (in December), and early in the morning and late in the afternoon.

Adventure Hiking (with map and compass)

Adventure hiking is always fun and the best kind of adventure usually comes by doing cross-country "orienteering." This means you must have an expert knowledge of the use of map and compass. In addition it should be the right kind of map and the right kind of compass.

The best map is a topographic map of your area prepared by the United States Geologic Survey. On this map one inch equals 1000 feet of terrain. Such a map may be purchased at a local office equipment or stationery store, a college book store, or from the Map Information Office of the United States Geological Survey, Washington 25, D.C. Ask for a copy of the Topographic Map Index Circular of your own state. This is in the form of a small map divided into areas called *quadrangles*. From this map you can select the quadrangle you need to order. You may order the desired map from either of the two following places:

WHAT ON EARTH

East of the Mississippi River — Geological Survey,
Distribution Section, Washington 25, D.C.

West of the Missippi River — Geological Survey,
Distribution Section, Denver, Colorado

From this map learn the symbols for such things as contour
lines which show elevation, streams, lakes, buildings,
churches, marshes, cemeteries, bench marks, etc.

With a pencil, locate on the map the places with which you
are familiar. These may be on hikes that you have taken,
places where you have camped, lakes and streams where
you have fished, etc.

The best compass is the one easiest to use and developed
for the sport of "Orienteering." This is the "Silva" compass
which is available in several price ranges and can be ordered
directly from the American Camping Association, Bradford
Woods, Martinsville, Indiana 46151. Directions for using come
with these compasses. Become familiar with their use before
trying an Orienteering game.

Now let's use the map and compass together on a hike.
Two or more hikers should always go together so that if there
should be an accident, one can help the other.

Select a starting point for the hike and mark this on your
map with a small X. Select and mark the destination with another X. Draw a pencil line between these two points.

Now place the edge of the compass so that it is along the
line which you have drawn. Turn the housing of the compass
until the North-South lines running through the housing are
parallel to the North-South lines of the map. The compass is
now set and the direction of travel in degrees may be read
directly from the compass housing. Follow this reading across
country to your selected destination.

A Silver Coin Hike —

To help become familiar with the use of the compass, try a silver coin hike. Cut a number of fake silver coins from the tops of tin cans. There should be one coin for each person taking part. Separate the persons taking part in the coin hike and place one of the coins at the feet of each. Give each person separate directions on small cards, listing compass readings and the distances to be walked. These might be as follows:

Card 1 — Compass reading   90 degrees — 30 steps
Compass reading 210 degrees — 30 steps
Compass reading 330 degrees — 30 steps

Card 2 — Compass reading   20 degrees — 40 steps
Compass reading 140 degrees — 40 steps
Compass reading 260 degrees — 40 steps

Card 3 — Compass reading   60 degrees — 35 steps
Compass reading 180 degrees — 35 steps
Compass reading 300 degrees — 35 steps

Other cards may be added remembering to start the first reading with less than 120 degrees, adding 120 degrees to each of the next two readings. The number of steps will be the same for each reading.

If the given courses are followed carefully, each person will return to the point from which he started and should find the coin lying at his feet when he has completed the course.

Weatherproof Your Maps

Rain, dirt, and constant handling are very hard on maps but they are easily protected from these hazards by the use of plastics in the form of bags, sheets, and sprays.

Folded road maps may be protected by placing them in plastic bags fastened at the necks with rubber bands.

WHAT ON EARTH

Maps that are to be carried rolled up are best protected by cutting plastic bags used in dry-cleaning to the right size, covering both sides of the map and sealing with plastic tape or masking tape.

Flat maps should be protected using a heavy plastic sheet such as comes in photo albums. Apply to both sides of the map and seal with plastic or masking tape.

Clear, acrylic-type sprays may be used to protect small maps to be used in the field, providing there is no printing on the back of the map. Such sprays often cause such printing to bleed or show through on the front making the map difficult to read. Try a small spot as a test before spraying the entire map.

Mount Valuable Maps on Cloth

Maps or charts which are used often, soon become ragged along the edges and worn out along the folds, making them hard to read. To keep them in good condition obtain a specially prepared material called "Chartex" from an art supply store. This is a cloth material with an adhesive backing and will enable you to prepare your valuable maps so that you may use them over and over again.

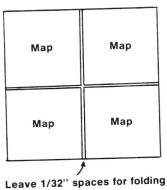

Leave 1/32" spaces for folding

Pioneers' Necessity

Cut the cloth backing material to a size about one inch larger than the map to be mounted.

Crease the map sharply at all folds, then carefully cut the map along each fold.

Starting with one corner of the map and using a warm iron, press the map onto the cloth backing, using a sheet of paper over the map to protect it from the iron. Place the second part of the map about 1/32 of an inch away from the first part. Press with the iron.

Continue until all parts of the map are in place with a 1/32 inch space between each part. These spaces are for folding the mounted map.

When all parts of the map have been mounted, use a straight edge and wooden block and trim the edges of the finished map with a sharp knife.

Smaller maps and charts may be mounted in one piece.

Now, how about building a small wooden case in which to keep these mounted maps and charts?

Hiking Hints

Plan the route of the hike in advance, but don't feel that you have to stick to it if something interesting appears along the way.

Be properly equipped, wearing good hiking shoes with good soles and pliable uppers. Dress warmly in the winter with several light layers of clothing that can be peeled off one at a time if you become too warm. Put clothing back on when you stop, for the body can cool off too fast.

Take along a compass and a U.S. Geologic Survey map of the area; also a small but adequate First Aid kit that you know how to use.

WHAT ON EARTH

Plan to have a hot meal on your hike. Prepare it in an aluminum foil pack the night before, perhaps with a large hamburger patty, potato strips, sliced carrot and onion rings. Add butter and salt to the package, wrap well and place in the freezer over night. In the morning, wrap the foil package in newspapers before placing in your pack. By lunch time it will be defrosted and ready to cook.

Gather "Squaw wood" (dead branches that you can break off a tree with your hands). Build a crisscross fire and let it burn down to a good bed of coals. Lay the foil package in the coals and cook for ten minutes on each side. Use a forked stick to turn the package over.

After eating, clean up the cooking-fire area and place the foil in your pack for disposal back home.

Carry a small plastic bag of "Bird seed" (a mixture of sugar-coated cereal, unsalted nuts, raisins, and M&M candies) for quick energy along the way.

Hiking in the Spring

Early spring is the finest time of year for hiking. Nature is being renewed. There is a feeling of new warmth in the air and the spring hiker cannot feel anything but enthusiasm. Birds and animals are at their happiest after a long winter.

So take to the woods and fields. If you have a gang, try some spring games to give added interest. Take along your topographic map and follow a pre-selected compass route to some selected spot. Try one of the following after you get there:

Art Gallery Orienteering—

In a convenient area close by, place 10 or more advertisements cut from magazines. Number each one. Starting with No. 1, add the compass reading to the next number's location. Give this reading plus the approximate distance to the next number on a small card located at each advertisement.

Give each hiker a pencil and paper and start them off singly a few minutes apart at #1. The compass reading at the last "art gallery" advertisement should take the hikers back to the starting point. The hikers are to list the advertisements in the order in which they have reached them.

To give some competition between groups, set up two similar courses using different advertisements for each. Divide the hikers into two groups with each group starting on a separate course at the same time. The first group back at the starting point with a complete list of advertisements, wins.

Camping in the Desert

Desert camping in the southwestern part of the United States is much different from the woodland camping in the East. But if you think it means nothing but camping on sand dunes, you are in for a big surprise. The western deserts are not desolate wastes of sand, but are filled with unusual trees, cacti, and other flowering plants; huge quantities of rocks of all kinds, and many birds, and other wildlife. This is the place for the rock hunter, the photographer, and the bird-watcher. There are plenty of trails for hiking and real excitement for any camper.

Two main items to be considered for desert camping are these:

   1—Bring all the water you will need.

   2—Stay on marked trails so you won't get lost.

Campers need at least one quart of water per day for drinking, plus additional water for cooking and washing. If meals are planned carefully and disposable dishes are used, dish washing may be almost eliminated.

Except for two or three weeks in the early spring there is little rain and tents are seldom needed. A poncho or fly will provide all of the shelter needed from the sun and possible showers.

Even though it seldom rains, never set up camp in a dry stream bed or narrow canyon for the little rain that does come may be so intense that you will be flooded out.

Nights are cool and even cold at times, so take along a sleeping bag or extra blankets. Blankets may also be used during the daytime to erect a shelter from the sun.

When your campsite has been selected, spread out your sleeping bag or blankets. Dig hip and shoulder holes to fit your body contours. When you are satisfied that you will be comfortable, roll up your sleeping gear again until ready for use at night. During the warm day lizards, bugs, and snakes may use it for shelter from the hot sun. During the cooler night, however, they are mostly inactive and you can expect to sleep in peace.

You will find plenty of fuel available in these deserts. Mesquite is probably the favorite fuel, but sagebrush and greasewood are good, as are the dead branches of the palo verde tree, cedar, yucca, and the dry parts of dead cacti such as cholla, ocatillo, and saguaro.

Drinking water may be obtained from the barrel cactus. Being careful of the sharp thorns, cut off the top of the cactus, remove the pulp from the inside and squeeze the sap into a container. The sap is nearly tasteless but refreshing. This cactus can also tell you the direction for nearly all barrel cacti lean towards the south.

Nearly all of the National Parks and Monuments have well-marked trails to be followed, either on foot or horseback.

Nights are even more exciting than the days in desert camping for at night there are millions of stars that seem to shine brighter and to be closer than anywhere else on earth, and the night sounds are much different, too. Go to sleep listening to the "lullaby" of the desert.

Camping in Wet Weather

Once upon a time, camping was an activity for warm, dry weather only but today it is part of the year-round program of many youth groups. Because of this it is important to gain "know-how" about wet-weather camping.

Here are a few pointers:

1. Select a safe, dry spot, never under trees where the water may continue to drip long after it has stopped raining. The dry spot will be on a slight elevation where the drainage is good and where the water will run away from, not toward, your tent.

2. Ditch your tent. This means digging a small ditch to carry water away as it drains from the sides of the tent. The ditch must be in the right spot to be of any value.

WHAT ON EARTH

That spot is directly beneath the edge of the tent so that water draining down the tent sides goes directly into the ditch. A ditch a few inches away from the edge of the tent is almost worthless.

3. Stakes should be driven deeper than normal when the ground is wet to provide greater holding power.

4. Collect plenty of dry wood. This will probably be dead branches broken from trees. Wood lying on the ground will be soaking wet while the dead branches, preferably without bark, found on the trees will at least be dry on the inside. Splitting these will provide reasonably dry wood that will burn well.

5. Collect a good fire-starter or tinder. The loose curly bark of the silver or grey birch contains an oil that burns well even when the bark is damp. Slivers cut from the inside of dead sumac, hemlock, or pine also make good tinder in wet weather. If possible, carry a good fire-starter with you in the form of candle stubs, rolled strips of paper or cardboard soaked in paraffin, or commercial fire-starters.

6. Hike with a poncho rather than a raincoat for this can be made to cover your pack as well as yourself. It also makes an excellent groundcloth to place beneath your sleeping bag or blankets.

7. Keep all equipment inside the tent and the sleeping bag or blankets rolled up until it is time to use them.

8. Erect a tarpaulin over the area for the campfire. As soon as a good fire is going, gather wood and allow it to dry in the heat of the fire.

9. Carry extra sugars and fats for food in cold, wet weather. They will provide extra energy and body warmth.

10. Build a reflector fire a few feet in front of your tent for warmth and comfort during the night.

11. Beware of rubbing against wet tent roofs. A leak may start in the spot where the wet canvas is rubbed.

12. Check tent ropes before going to bed. They shrink in wet weather and may need to be loosened to prevent tent stakes being pulled out during the night. Be sure to tighten them again when the weather becomes good.

Winter Camp-Out Hints

Pick a campsite sheltered by evergreens or on the opposite side of a hill from the prevailing winds.

Use open-front Baker or Explorer tents with a reflector fire in front.

To sleep warm, be sure to have as much underneath as over you. An air mattress, placed on a few newspapers will insulate your bed. An insulated sleeping bag with one or more light blankets is better than heavy blankets.

WHAT ON EARTH

Keep winter meals high in calories with plenty of fats and sugars. Use stews, hot cereals, bacon and eggs for main meals.

Stay warm by keeping on the move. Cutting wood gives double warmth, once while doing the cutting and again when the wood is burned.

When You are Lost in the Woods

Best of all, make sure that you do not get lost in the first place, but sometime this may happen in spite of ourselves. To make certain that you can find your way out of the woods, here are some things to do and not to do.

First of all, before going out in the woods in unfamiliar territory, obtain a Geologic Survey map of the area and spend some time studying it. Learn the principle features and landmarks of the area. Take this map, a compass and a loud whistle with you on your hike.

If you should find that you are lost, do these things:

1. Sit down and think. Stay put for a while and, if it is cold, gather wood and start a fire. Someone will certainly come looking for you sooner or later and you might as well be comfortable while you wait. If it is late in the day, plan to stay in that spot overnight. Gather enough wood to keep your fire going all night.

2. Use your whistle. Blow an S O S every few minutes. If you don't know the Morse Code, blow three long blasts occasionally to guide anyone searching for you.

3. Find shelter among evergreen trees or in a sheltered area, particularly if it looks like a long stay.

4. If help hasn't come after several hours, get out the map and compass. Lay the map on the ground and place the compass on top of the map. Now turn the map until the *north* sign on the map is pointing the

same way as the needle of the compass. From the general topography of the area you should be able to tell your approximate location on the map. Now, with the map oriented with the compass, read the direction in degrees that you will have to walk to get back to familiar territory. Check frequently with the compass to keep on a reasonably straight course until there is some landmark from which you can determine your actual position on the map.

Keep your compass tied to your clothing to prevent its loss.

On the way out, take your time. Walk, don't run, helping to prevent an accident that might compound your troubles.

EARTH'S WATERS—PROVIDE FOOD

When, Where and How to Fish

The pioneers learned by necessity that you don't need fancy equipment to catch fish. A pole or rod, a good fish line, an assortment of fishhook sizes, a piece of leader, a float, assorted sinkers, and bait are all that are needed.

Learn to tie the right kind of knots in your line and leaders and to attach hooks in the proper manner. (See pages 62 to 63.)

The best times for bait fishing are early morning and late afternoon. Just before a storm is also good but don't stay on the water until a storm becomes bad. Watch for jumping fish and for sudden swirls on the surface of the water. These are signs that fish are feeding.

When the weather is hot, fish the cool spots where the water is deep and shaded. In cool weather, fish the warmer shallow water.

Fish particularly like to stay at the head of a riffle, in small rapids, and in the eddies below rocks and logs, under overhanging bushes and trees, and among submerged weeds, brush, and rocks.

For bait use worms, small minnows, parts of shellfish, insects, or parts of fish. When a fish has been caught, open its stomach and see what it has been eating. If possible, collect more of this food and use it as bait for other fish.

Making Primitive Fishing Tackle

It is still possible to make your own hooks and lines using the methods developed by the Indians and other primitive people. Using this homemade tackle successfully is a real adventure and is very satisfying. Why not try it?

For materials, collect a variety of thorns from such trees as the thorn-apple, honey-locust, cactus and other thorn-bearing trees and plants.

WHAT ON EARTH

Follow the illustrations shown and you can easily make effective hooks, lines, and spears.

Other materials which may be used are bone, wood, shells, pins, needles, and wire.

For lines, use the inner bark of the basswood, Indian hemp, mulberry, yucca, milkweed or other fiber-producing plant materials.

Making fishline—

To make line, gather the inner bark of one of the above materials and shred the fibers into long narrow strips. Soaking the bark in advance helps. Shredding may be done by laying the bark over a log and pounding it gently with a stick until the fibers separate.

Taking two long strips of the bark, tie them together at one end. Holding one strand in each hand just below the place where they are tied, twist the strand in the right hand in a clockwise direction. Place this twisted strand across the front of the other strand and change hands. The untwisted strand will now be in the right hand. Twist this strand in the same clockwise motion and lay it across the top of the other strand again changing hands. Since the strands are twisted in one direction and then laid across the other strand in the opposite direction, they will not come untwisted.

As you approach the ends of the strands of bark, add another strand of bark three or four inches from the end. Twist this addition with the original strand and continue as before.

The strength of this homemade fishline depends upon the kind of bark used, the number of fibers used for one strand, and the care taken in rolling and twisting. A detailed description of this process may be found in the book, CREATIVE NATURE CRAFTS by R. O. Bale, published by the Burgess Publishing Co., Minneapolis 15, Minnesota.

Making Spears —

Make fish spears from bamboo poles, either with their own barbed points, or add bone or metal barbs and points.

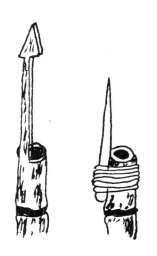

WHAT ON EARTH

Making Fishhooks—

Fishhooks may be made from a variety of materials found in nature.

A thorn fishhook—

Whittle a 2½''-3'' shaft from a small twig. Cut a small notch in one end of the twig and trim the end of a thorn to an angle that will fit this notch.

Bind the thorn tightly to the shaft with cordage made from native materials, with thread or even with a raveling taken from clothing. Cross the strands several times, binding the shaft both above and below the notch where the thorn is attached.

A second smaller thorn may be attached in a notch at the upper end of the shaft, projecting towards the point of the first thorn, but with the point of the smaller thorn inside and slightly above the point of the larger thorn. The purpose of this second thorn is to keep fish from slipping off the hook made by the first thorn. Tie or bind the fishline to the upper end of the hook.

Briar fishhooks—

A fishhook may be made from a piece of vine or bush having briars. Look for a vine having both briars and stem in the shape illustrated. Trim to size and attach the line to the center of this hook. Bait and use as mentioned above.

A gorge Fishhook —

To make a gorge fishhook, trim a piece of hardwood about ¼" in diameter and ¾-1 inch in length, into the shape illustrated having two sharp points and a notch around the center for attaching the fishline.

To catch a fish the gorge must be swallowed completely. This normally is most effective during darkness. Attach a bait of pieces of shellfish, pieces of fish or meat, or worms and then tie the line to a branch overhanging the water so that the branch will bend and keep tension on the line when a fish is caught.

A wishbone fishhook —

Use a wishbone from a chicken or other bird of similar size. Turkey wishbones may be used to make large fishhooks. Use a sharp knife or file to trim one side of the wishbone into a short, barbed hook shaped as nearly as possible like a regular metal fishhook. (See illustration).

To use with these primitive types of fishing tackle, cut a slender branch from a tree, or fish with a hand line.

WHAT ON EARTH

Tying the Right Knot in Fishing Tackle —

If a knot comes untied when you are in the process of landing a big fish, you may become very disgusted with yourself. To make certain that you know how to tie fishline together properly, to a swivel, to a leader, or to a hook, practice tying the following illustrated knots until you can tie them easily. Practice with a piece of cotton clothesline or sashcord and then you will find it easier when you work with fine braided or monofilament line. Remember that the knots are the weakest points in your fishline. A 6 lb.-test line will not take nearly that weight of pull if the knots are improperly tied.

The clincher knot:

This is the correct knot used to attach a line to a swivel, flies, or artificial lures. Following the illustration, place the line through the swivel or lure; bring the short end of the line back and twist five times around the standing part of the fishline. Thread the short end back through the first loop just above the eye of the swivel or lure and then back through the long loop which you have just made in passing through the eye.

Pull the main or standing part of the line to close the knot tightly on the eye.

The Clincher Knot

The dropper knot:

Occasionally you may wish to add a second or third hook somewhere above the end of the line. For this we use the dropper knot. Form a loop in the line at the point where you wish to attach the second hook. (See illustration). Twist the free end of the line twice around the first part of the inside of the loop. Spread the twist after the second turn and pull the single part of the loop through the spread. Pull on both the free end and the main part of the line to tighten the knot. Add a hook or leader to the loop you have made.

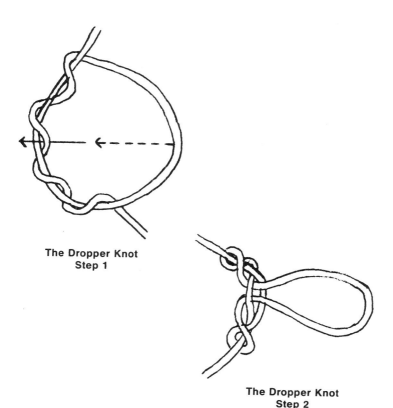

The Dropper Knot
Step 1

The Dropper Knot
Step 2

WHAT ON EARTH

The perfection knot:

> This is used to tie a leader to the hook, to the lure, or to the line. Pass the leader through the eye or loop to which it is being attached. Form a loop by passing the short end once around the main part of the line. Bring the short end down and pass it through the first twist around the main part of the line, passing over the main line and then back beneath itself. (This is much easier than it sounds. See the illustration.)

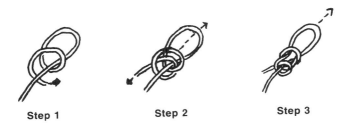

Step 1   Step 2   Step 3

The blood knot:

> This is the correct knot to use in joining two lines. Overlap the two free ends about 3 inches. Twist each end five times around the other. Bring both free ends back to the center of the twist and pass them through between the two lines. Tighten by pulling on both of the long standing lines. Trim off the free ends.

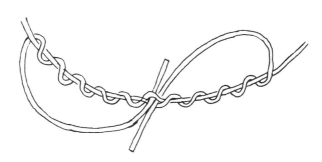

Grow or Make Your Own Fish Bait

When the fishing is the best, bait is usually the hardest to find. Lick this problem by growing your own or preserving it so that you will have it ready when needed.

Worms—

Angleworms and nightcrawlers are favorites. Make sure they are available by having a special spot where they like to stay. Pick a well-fertilized spot in the garden or chicken yard or close to a livestock barn. In this spot dig a deep hole and fill it with well-rotted barnyard manure or leaf mold mixed with a small amount of ordinary dirt. A 3 by 3 ft. hole 2 or 3 feet deep will be fine. Keep this area damp, not wet, and occasionally sprinkle a little moistened corn meal, crumbs or bacon drippings over the area.

Worms will soon move into this moist area where food is easily available.

Dig for them as needed, using a spading fork rather than a shovel so as not to cut the worms in two.

If you get tired of digging, try this suggestion:

Mix one tablespoon of mustard into one quart of water. When the soil is moist, sprinkle this mustard solution on the surface of the ground and then wait for worms to emerge so you can pick them up. The mustard solution makes the skin smart and the worms will soon come to the surface. Pick them up and wash them well in clear water then use them for bait.

Preserving Minnows—

Net a number of small minnows. Place the minnows in layers of salt in an open crock or other container for 4 to 5 days, pouring out all moisture as it collects and adding more salt as needed. In use, these salted minnows will freshen on your hook and will last as well as bait.

WHAT ON EARTH

Doughballs for Catfish and Carp —

Mix equal parts of flour, cornmeal, and shredded cotton with enough water to make a thick dough. Add a small amount of strong grated cheese. Shape into doughballs about ½ inch in diameter and cook in boiling water for about 20 minutes. Dry and cool the doughballs, place them in plastic bags or boxes and store them in the refrigerator until they're needed.

Frozen Baits —

Crayfish, pieces of chicken intestines, minnows, clams, etc. may be placed in small containers and quick-frozen. Thaw them out for use as needed. Small green and brown smooth-skinned worms may also be collected and frozen in plastic bags to which a little cold water has been added.

Collect meal worms and other larvae, place them in a small jar of moist cornmeal and store them in the refrigerator.

Pork Rind Baits —

Cut strips from pork rinds and string them on fishhooks like worms.

Raise Crickets for Fish Bait

It's fun to raise your own bait and it is also profitable if you can raise it for sale.

Start the project by building a cricket-raising box. It can be of any size and should have a screened top (window screening).

For each square foot of bottom space in the box, collect five male and five female crickets. How can you tell them apart? The females have long egg-laying tubes extending from their abdomens.

Place the crickets in the box and add food and water as well as a place for laying their eggs. A very small amount of poultry laying-mash makes an excellent food for crickets.

Use baby chick drinking fountains to hold drinking water. To prevent drowning, fill the base of the fountain with cotton or small pebbles.

An egg laying box is made from a shallow pan filled with moist (not wet) clean sand, placed in the bottom of the box.

In cold weather, the addition of an electric light will provide heat to keep the crickets active.

Mature crickets can be separated from those too small for bait by placing the crickets in a tin can covered with ¼ inch mesh screen. Suspend the can upside down and the smaller crickets will crawl through the screen.

How To Use Worms As Fish Bait

Angleworms are the nearest universal bait for all kinds of fish - bass, rainbow trout, brook trout, lake trout, pickerel, pike, perch, bluegills, bullheads, and even the great sturgeon. Worms are the natural fish food, especially after storms when they are washed into the streams and lakes.

Other kinds of worms are also excellent bait, but the most common worms used for fish bait are the ordinary garden angleworms and nightcrawlers.

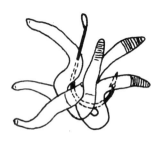

Bullheads, catfish, and bass go for clusters of worms.

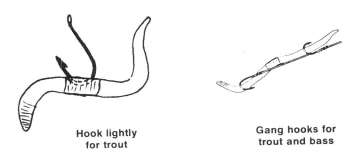

**Hook lightly
for trout**

**Gang hooks for
trout and bass**

Fish may leave artificial baits as soon as they have touched them for they are normally without taste. However, most fish are reluctant to leave natural foods that have taste, odor, and action, provided the hook and line are properly concealed. They will take worms any time of the day or year.

The type of fishing tackle is not important when you are worm fishing but the method of hooking the worm is of prime importance.

Floats or bobbers attached 4 - 5 feet from the end of the line are fine for those who want to relax while fishing. If the fish do not bite at this depth, try other depths. Sometimes a change of a foot or so in the fishing depth makes a great deal of difference.

If you are using a monofilament line, no leader is needed, but if the line is a braided type, there should be 2 to 3 feet of transparent leader attached between the end of the line and the hook. This leader should be 4 to 6 lb. test.

If a sinker is used, it should be light enough so that the float or bobber stays on top of the water. If no bobber is used, a heavier sinker may be in order. Attach the sinker 2 to 3 feet from the hook. Sometimes the leader is extended below the hook, with the sinker attached 2 to 3 feet below the bait.

Make Your Own Spinning Lures

You can purchase your lures, but it is more fun if you can catch fish on lures that you have made yourself. Try some of the following. After you have made one or more, you may wish to try your own variations or even design some yourself. Most of the needed supplies are available at sporting goods stores, but a lot of them may be improvised.

Spoons — used for casting or trolling

> Cut the bowl from a stainless steel teaspoon. If it seems too large, draw the outline you wish on the spoon with a pencil and then file or grind to the right shape. (A power sander or grinder is fine for this purpose.)

> Drill small holes (about 1/16 inch) at each end of the spoon. At one end, which should be a little more pointed than the other, attach a treble hook using a split ring.

> At the opposite end attach a swivel and leader using another split ring.

WHAT ON EARTH

Spinners—used for casting or trolling

Drill lengthways through a one inch long lead sinker, or remove the wire center from a sinker having wire ends.

Using piano wire, run the wire through the sinker, through a small glass bead (from old costume jewelry) and attach it to a small brass swivel.

Attach a treble hook to the swivel with a split ring.

Run the opposite end of the piano wire through a second glass bead and then through a tiny spinner blade cut from a piece of bright tin, or use the spinner from old broken fishing tackle. Add another glass bead and attach it to a second swivel.

Surface Plugs—for casting

Cut 2 to 3 inch plugs from a broom handle, hardwood dowels, clothespins, etc., and shape as illustrated; then sand smooth. (I prefer ½ inch dowels.)

Attach a treble hook to the smaller end using a small screw eye if available. Add a second small screw eye to the larger end and a brass swivel, using a split ring to attach it. Paint the plug with several coats of airplane dope, rubbing each coat smooth with fine steel wool.

(If small screw eyes are not available, drill lengthwise through the plug with a 1/16 inch drill before shaping, then run copper wire through this drilled hole and attach the hook and swivel to the wire.)

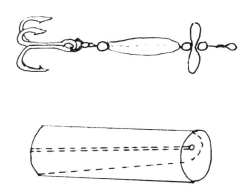

Underwater Plugs—for either casting or trolling

Construct plugs similar to the surface plugs above. Drill a hole in the center of the underside of the plug and fill it with lead. The correct amount of lead is just enough so that the plug will sink to a depth of ten feet in ten seconds. The amount will depend upon the size of the plug you have made. Experiment until the amount is just about right.

Insert lead plug

To fill the drilled hole with lead, cut small pieces of lead from an old sinker and force them into the hole with a hammer and nailset. Sand or file the surface smooth.

WHAT ON EARTH

Repairing Your Fishing Gear

Fishhooks should be sharpened regularly to keep them sharp-pointed to insure hooking that fish. Use a small regular sharpening stone carried in your tackle box.

Flies that look battered and out of condition can have their fluffiness restored by holding them in the steam from a teakettle for a minute or two.

Polish fishing spoons with a good chrome metal cleaner. Wipe them dry and dip them in clear lacquer to prevent tarnish and rust.

Clean and oil your fishing reel regularly, especially the level-wind mechanism.

Reset loose ferrules on your rod. Cement them in place then wind with silk thread and cover the silk with colorless nail polish.

Fishing For Bass

Bass are hard hitting fish and a real thrill to catch. Watch a bass hit a surface plug and you may see it knock the plug into the air for several feet, catching it again on the way down. This may be an attempt to stun the bait but gives an added thrill when you see it happen.

It is interesting to note that many fish make nests. Among the bass it is the male who builds the nest of stones cleaned of all sediment. The female bass lays her sticky eggs on the clean stones of the nest, but it is the male bass who guards the eggs, remaining almost motionless over the nest while fanning the eggs steadily with his fins.

Bass are attracted to floating plugs, surface lures, underwater plugs and spoons, live bait and many artificial baits which resemble the natural bass foods such as frogs, minnows, and crawfish. They may be attracted to weird creations which are like nothing found in nature. Striped, spotted, or plain, they are very effective. Noisy surface lures may bubble, gurgle, or splash and seem to have an unusual attraction for bass.

Floating plugs and lures have the added attraction of being able to dodge the snags that are often present under water. They may be reeled in across these submerged hazards just as long as there is enough water to float them above the potential snags.

Surface lures for bass vary from small cork or deer-hair bugs designed for light rods, to the heavier plugs used with heavier tackle.

The attractiveness of lures for bass may change from hour to hour, and what was most effective at one time, has no effect at others. For this reason the wise bass fisherman will carry a good assortment of lures.

Surface lures work best in comparatively shallow waters, up to about 15 feet deep and may work best in lakes, ponds, and quiet spots in rivers. Bass in these shallow places normally do not stay in open water but like the concealment of sunken trees, brush, lily pads, weed beds, and submerged rocks. When bass refuse to take surface lures, try underwater plugs, spoons, and live bait. However, it is the surface lure that provides the most fun in bass fishing.

WHAT ON EARTH

In casting, place the lure as close as possible to the places where bass may hide, leaving the lure motionless at the spot where it lands until the ripples have subsided. Then twitch the lure for only an inch or two. Let it lie still for a moment more and then reel it in slowly. Bass will often strike while the lure is lying motionless. If this method doesn't work, change to another lure and reel in a little faster.

In bass fishing, the fisherman should keep low down in the boat or on the shore and avoid making noise.

Catfish and Bullhead Fishing

There are nearly 1000 species in the catfish family; those fish with the long "whiskers." All of the species, however, are much alike in their habits and an understanding of those habits is what helps us to catch them.

All members of the catfish family are bottom-feeders. Their "whiskers" are covered with taste buds and with them they are able to follow a "taste" through the water. As bottom-feeders they are constantly nosing around through the mud, weeds, brush, and other debris looking for dead crawfish, minnows, and anything that is edible. In spite of its food, the catfish or bullhead is delicious eating. It s bottom-feeding habit tells us where to fish for it and perhaps the kind of bait to use.

Catfish and bullheads live in lakes, ponds, and rivers. The larger catfish are found in rivers in the South and West while the smaller-sized bullheads are usually found in the smaller ponds, lakes, and backwaters of streams. The four common species of catfish found in North America are the "channel catfish," averaging upwards of four pounds but sometimes running up to fifty or more pounds in weight, small head, forked tail, silver-white with spots on its sides; the "blue catfish," blue-grey in color, small head, forked tail and weighing up to ninety pounds; the "flathead catfish" with a large head, square tail, and dark grey in color, running from 5-25 pounds; and the "bullhead," dark grey to black and running from ½ to 1 pound.

For the smaller fish you will normally need a No. 4 fishhook, varying with the average size of the fish you catch. Carry a small whetstone with you and keep the hook sharpened to a needle point.

Baits for catfish and bullheads consist of nightcrawlers (large clusters of them for the large varieties), liver, pieces of dead fish, dead minnows, and other forms of dead water-life.

The catfish and bullhead are wary feeders and often "mouth" the bait before taking it completely. If they feel the pull of a sinker or rod, they are apt to drop the bait and leave it alone thereafter. To prevent this use a barrel sinker, one with a hole through the center, through which the line may slide freely. Six to twelve inches above the hook, tie a small piece of wood just large enough to keep the barrel sinker from sliding over it. The sinker should be above this point. When the fish mouths the bait and gives it a tug, the line will slide through the sinker and the fish can swallow the bait without the warning pull of the sinker to stop him. Let the fish run with the bait until he stops. Then, set the hook.

If the hook is very far down the fish's throat, don't try to get it out until the fish is dressed. Just cut the line and use another hook until this one can be recovered.

WHAT ON EARTH

During the day a float may be used to show when the bait has been swallowed. At night, fish without a float so that the pull of the bait can be felt and the hook set.

All catfish and bullheads must be handled with care to prevent painful wounds and infection that comes from the slime covering the fish's body. Wounds are caused by three sharp fins, two pectoral fins on the sides and the dorsal fin on the back. These are sharp-pointed and sometimes barbed. In handling catfish and bullheads wear gloves while removing the hook or use wire cutters or kitchen shears to cut off the sharp points of these three fins before handling.

Perch Fishing

These small, pretty, striped fish are delicious. They do not seem to be afraid of noise or commotion and are often seen the hottest days, resting in the shadow of your boat. It will take several for a good meal so don't worry about catching too many. The perch is one of the most prolific of fish with a single female producing up to a quarter of a million eggs in a single season.

Favorite baits are earthworms, small minnows, or even the tough part of chicken gizzards. The only tackle needed is pole and line, float and hook, but you may want to try some refinements for more sport. Try a light rod and a very light monofilament line with a small float that will show the slightest nibble. Use split-shot sinkers that will put your bait, worms, pieces of gizzard, or small wet-flies down on the bottom. If you have spinning equipment, use small metal spoons or spinners that sink a few feet beneath the surface.

Once perch are caught, prepare them for eating by slicing through the skin and flesh along both sides of the backbone, cutting carefully along the outside of the ribs. Remove the meat sections with the skin from each side of the body, then grasp the skin at the tail end with a pair of pliers, sliding a knife under the skin and trimming the flesh from the skin leaving a strip of fillet ready to fry. If this proves too difficult, scale the perch before removing the meat sections from the ribs and fry with the skin on.

Dip in finely ground cornmeal and fry in butter, two or three minutes on each side.

Muskelunge Fishing

If you have fished for days trying to catch the murderous-looking muskelunge, try fishing for him at night. Start just about dusk and, if you can stay awake, fish until just after daybreak. Use lures that stay on the surface and are noisy, the noisier the better, and fish them very, very slowly. The color of the lures make little difference, but the amount of noise and disturbance the lures make is important.

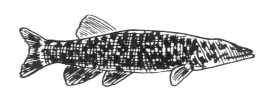

For musky fishing, use a rod with plenty of stiffness and a line that is heavy but easily cast. Try a 20 to 25 pound line. A light line may be more sporting, but it is easily broken and the musky may be left with your plug lodged in his throat. You have lost the plug and the fish will probably die.

If they are not biting at night, try the harder fishing spots in the daytime. These are the weedy areas, using weedless plugs, spoons, or pork rinds. Try trolling with large, live minnows or still-fish in the deep holes with large minnows or frogs. Another method of trolling is to use a floating plug with a heavy enough sinker placed about two feet in front of it to drag on the bottom, leaving the plug floating behind it.

Fish the spots where you have had good luck before. When you have caught one, move to another spot until a second musky has had a chance to move into the vacant area, then try again in the same place. Where one is found, there will be another later on, for these are favorite spots.

The musky is not too particular about what he eats. Suckers and perch are regular food, but he will also eat young ducks, mice, birds flying just above the water, and almost any other animal within his size limit.

The larger bass lures, especially those active under the surface of the water such as spoons, plugs, poppers, streamers, and large flies are often effective during daylight hours. Use large surface lures, especially at night and on calmer waters.

Use a stainless steel leader 12 to 15 inches long, both for bait-casting and trolling.

Once the musky is hooked, give him line when he wants it, but keep it snug. Be sure the boat is unanchored and ready to follow him when he gets to the end of your line. Don't be in a hurry to get him into the boat. Tire him out as long as he shows signs of fighting and don't be afraid to use a small club on his head before bringing him into the boat for a live musky can do a lot of damage.

Ice Fishing

Ice fishing is a chilly sport but if you are catching fish you won't mind it. Ice fishing is often the cure for winter-time blues that come when active people are confined too long. It is also the time when the fish that were overfed last summer are hungrily looking for something to eat. This is why you are more apt to catch your limit in the winter.

Expensive equipment is not needed but before you start making or buying equipment, find out what fish are legal during the winter months in your state and don't forget to carry your fishing license with you.

Among the fish that bite readily during the winter are perch, pickerel, walleyed pike, bluegills, bass, trout, whitefish, and smelt. Others may bite too, when it is not too cold.

Almost any lake or pond with clean water and with deep holes or channels should provide good fishing. Try the main channels in the larger rivers and the quiet bends in the rivers also, making certain that the ice has frozen to a safe thickness.

For safety on smaller lakes and ponds, be sure that there is at least six inches of good ice. The larger lakes and rivers should have at least a foot of solid ice. The smaller lakes and ponds will provide good fishing before the ice is thick enough for safety on the larger ones.

Shallow lakes and ponds covered with ice and snow may have so limited a supply of oxygen that fish are sluggish or may die during the long winter months. The best fishing is in deep lakes, ponds, and streams where there is little snow and a few open spots where the water has not frozen.

Clear ice is not always the best for winter fishing for the fish may be disturbed by movement and shadows from above. Select a spot where there is a little snow or where the ice is cloudy. When you find such a place, cut a hole through the ice where fish may be attracted to the light that streams through the hole. The weather and the time of day have comparatively little effect on the chances of fish biting during the winter. The best time for ice fishing is when you have the time for it.

Ice fishing on large lakes has other hazards than just thin ice. One of these is the danger of snow squalls that makes vision very poor. For this reason plan to carry a compass when fishing far from shore. Before starting to fish, take a compass reading of the direction you will want to follow if a sudden storm develops.

Equipment needed-

Use a wooden sled to carry your equipment. Attach a long rope for towing the sled and to use for lifesaving in case of emergency. The sled should be one that will float and the rope should be long enough to throw to a person who may have broken through thin ice.

Wear warm clothing because ice fishing is not a vigorous sport and the body easily becomes chilled. Insulated under wear and warm socks are important. Insulated boots or shoe pacs are excellent provided insulated socks or two pair of woolen socks are worn with them. Windproof outer clothing including a windproof hood should be a part of your outfit Wear the hood over a knitted hat or woolen cap with ea flaps. Woolen mittens with warm liners are essential and wi keep the fingers warmer than gloves. Handwarmers using liquid fuel are desirable. Be sure to take a pair of good sı glasses for your eyes can soon tire from the glare of sun the ice and snow.

Fit the sled with a wooden box to carry your fishing tə and the following items that help provide comfort:

A lantern or portable heater. Placed in the wooden ı while fishing, this provides a way of quickly warming hands.

A canvas wind-screen that can be attached to the sled or box using a light wooden frame set into sockets on the sled or box; or use a small, easily-erected tent that can be set by or over the fishing hole cut through the ice. A canvas and frame wind-screen should be at least 6 x 6 ft. and an even larger size may be desirable to provide shelter from two directions, for the wind often changes. If the wind-screen needs to be anchored, carry some weights for this purpose, or cut small holes in the ice, pour in some water and let the anchors freeze in place.

An ice spud, chisel, or ice auger for cutting fishing holes. Make or buy a 4 to 5 ft. spud made from a heavy iron bar having a chisel-shaped cutting end. Fasten a cord or leather loop to the dull end and loop this around the wrist while cutting the hole to prevent accidental loss of the spud. An ice auger makes holes quicker and easier than a spud but will probably cost more. Get a size about 6 inches in diameter. This is large enough for ice fishing. Most beginners make the fishing holes too large.

An axe is a poor tool for cutting ice holes because, once the hole is a few inches deep, the position of the axe handle makes it almost impossible to go deeper.

The right tackle-

Tackle may be very simple. A good strong handline, wound on a slat one foot long and notched at both ends will make it easy to measure the length of line let down through the hole.

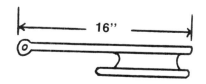

WHAT ON EARTH

This is important for fish usually stay at a particular depth during the winter. The handline should be relatively thick so that it can be handled easily while wearing mittens. Use a few feet of monofilament line at the end of the handline.

Make yourself a jigging stick similar to the diagram. This can be held in the hand and used as a small rod, or it may be used as a tip-up rig. A small wooden dowel, placed across the hole, will provide a pivot for the jigging stick permitting the reel end of the stick to tip up when a fish tugs at the bait.

If you are fishing several holes some distance apart, try providing each hole with a small sapling fish rod about 5 ft. in length. Cut a small gouge in the ice near each fishing hole, place the larger end of the sapling in the hole at a 45 degree angle with the smaller end of the sapling directly above the fishing hole. Pour some water around the base of the sapling and allow it to freeze in place. Split the smaller end of each sapling for an inch or two and run the handline through the slot. Attach a piece of colored cloth so that when a fish takes the bait, motion of the cloth will attract the fisherman. If a single hole is being fished, a hand-held line is more fun, for the fisherman then has direct contact with the fish.

If you have a problem with your line freezing on the reel, you may want to purchase or make a wet-reel type of tip-up. You may even suspend the reel in the water. The name "tip-up" comes from the design of the fishing rig which either tips or releases a spring moving a colored flag when a fish takes the bait. The wet-reel is made to keep the reel below the surface of the water where it will not freeze.

An easily made tip-up consists of two small pieces of scrap lumber fastened together in the shape of a cross. The two longer ends of the cross are placed across the hole in the ice. Attach a small red flag to one of the shorter arms of the cross. The other arm is placed with the end directly over the center of the fishing hole and the fishing line is attached to this end. A fish, tugging on the bait, will cause the cross to tip, raising the flag to make the fisherman aware of the action.

A rough but effective tip-up can be made from a small sapling having branches on opposite sides.

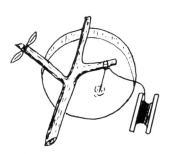

Before putting out a string of tip-ups be sure to check the laws to see if there is a limit to the number of tip-ups one fisherman is permitted.

What kind of bait?-

Check with other ice fishermen to see what kinds of bait they are finding effective. Try these for yourself:

Live minnows	Small pieces of liver
Pork rinds	Artificial fish eggs
Maggots	Fish eyes
Grubs	

How about hooks?-

Use small hooks (Nos. 6 and 8 are good). Attach split-shot sinkers 18 to 24 inches above the hook for shallower waters and heavier sinkers where you are fishing deeper. The advantage of the heavier sinker is that it gets the bait down quicker and will also pull the line through slush ice if the hole keeps freezing over.

Hints for the beginner-

Fish close to the bottom. Let the line down until the sinker touches bottom and then raise it a few inches.

WHAT ON EARTH

If artificial lures are used or the bait is motionless, use a gentle jigging action to give motion to the bait.

Perch, bluegills, bass, and pickerel are more often found in shallow water (6 to 15 ft.). Lake trout and whitefish are usually found at a depth of more than 30 ft.

Strikes are not nearly as hard in the winter as in the summer and may be felt as merely gentle tugs on the handline.

Live minnows should be kept where they will not freeze. Cut an extra hole and suspend your minnow bucket in the water with a stick through the bail to keep it from sinking to the bottom.

Cooking Fish In Camp

Before going fishing, do a little practice casting in your backyard. Try placing an old tire or innertube on the ground and then casting to place the fly, plug, or spoon inside the tire. When you can do this 90% of the time you are getting pretty good at it.

Then when you go fishing, be optimistic and take along the things you will need for cleaning and cooking your catch. Chances are you will need them.

Fish never taste better than when they are caught and cooked as soon as possible.

Five ways of preparing fish in the out-of-doors are planking, frying, poaching, steaming, and smoking. Planking is probably the least known way and yet one of the best.

Planking Fish —

Cut off the head, slit down the back and through the ribs close to both sides of the backbone. Remove the backbone and clean, washing both the inside and outside of the fish well.

Cut a few seasoned hardwood pegs about 3/16 inch in diameter and about 3 inches long. Use these to nail the cleaned fish, flesh-side out, to a clean plank or section of log to be propped in front of the fire. Move the plank closer to, or farther from, the fire to regulate the heat. Add a little salt when the fish is nearly done. Eat, using your fingers, as soon as the fish is done, if you can wait that long.

Frying Fish—

Fry the fish in a frypan over hot coals, using a small amount of butter, oleo, shortening, or bacon fat. Turn the fish over two or three times as it cooks. Add salt to taste.

Poaching Fish—

Poaching means cooking in a small amount of water. Use one half to one cup of water to which a tablespoon of vinegar has been added. Cook in frypan over hot coals until done. Salt to taste.

Steaming Fish—

This method is particularly effective for the smaller trout you may have caught. Prepare a good bed of hot coals— no flames are wanted for this. Cut as many green sticks as you have fish. They should be about 18 inches long and as large around as your thumb. Tie the trout, one to a stick, near the smaller end of the stick, tying at the base of the tail. Push the opposite end of the stick into the coals until the head of the trout is partially covered. Steam for 10 to 15 minutes or until the flesh is flaky and tender. After cooking, remove the meat from the fish and discard the rest.

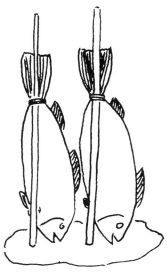

Smoke Your Fish —

Small fish provide little food when cleaned and fried, but just try smoking them and you may never go back to any other method of preparing fish.

Smoking requires pickling the fish first. For this you will need

Brown Sugar
Salt
Some sort of smoker

Clean the fish, leaving the heads on. Prepare the pickling mixture using equal parts of brown sugar and salt, planning on 1 lb. of each for a half dozen small fish.

Stir the mixture thoroughly and then rub as much as possible into the fish both inside and outside. Pack the fish with this mixture in a plastic bag or dish and allow to stand for about 12 hours. They are then ready to be smoked.

The smoker is a wooden box, open at the top and bottom and with a short piece of stovepipe having an elbow at one end, running into the bottom of the box. A trough may be dug into a small earth bank and the pipe placed in this trough and the box placed over the open end of the pipe. The elbow extends out of the trough and is turned downward over the spot where a smoky fire is to be built. The pipe should slant downward from the box to the fire so that the draft will draw the smoke upwards through the box.

When the fish have been pickled for about 12 hours, string them by the heads on a stiff wire and suspend them inside the wooden box, placing a loose cover over the box.

Under the open elbow of the pipe, start a fire using hickory wood and keep it going slowly for the next 12 hours. this is the same wood used for smoking the best hams.

When the smoking has progressed for about 12 hours, sample the fish. It will be so good, you may never want it any other way.

WHAT ON EARTH

Another method of smoking fish in camp is this—

Use a large pot having a cover.

Clean the fish leaving on the skin, fins and tails.

Cut slender green sticks, one per fish, and long enough to reach across the pot. Push a stick through each fish near the base of the tail and hang the fish in the pot in which you have placed about two inches of red cedar twigs. Cover the pot as well as you can and place it over a fire for about one hour. When done, discard the tough skin, eating the well cooked and smoked flesh.

Part 3

MAKE THE MOST

OF NATURE

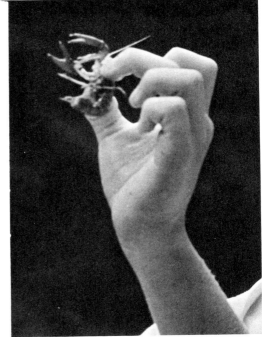

STREAM EXPLORING

When you are ready to take a little time out from fishing, try stream exploring. Take a good look under stones and debris in the stream, beneath overhanging banks, on trees and bushes having branches hanging in the water, and in the air above the stream.

You may not know what you are looking for until you find it but you will find many different kinds of life that you may not have known existed. A little snooping may give you some ideas for new fish baits too, baits that the fish knew well but that were unknown to you.

Look for the homes of caddis flies. They are found on the under sides of stones, logs, and branches and are made of a variety of materials glued together into small cylinders in which the caddis fly larvae live. Between one and two inches in length, they may be made of tiny twigs, grasses, sand, or gravel glued together by a liquid from the mouth of the larvae. Occasionally, the larvae can be seen playing an apparent game of tag with one entering the rear of a tube-shaped home forcing another larva out of the front. This one will immediately go in through the rear door forcing out the first intruder. This will continue time after time until they tire of the activity.

When they reach the end of the larval state, they will seal up both ends of their tubes and become pupae. Late in the pupal stage they will develop a set of powerful jaws with which they cut a new exit and crawl out of the tube onto a rock or plant stem where they dry out their new wings and begin life as adult caddis flies having long antennae bending backwards over their glossy wings.

Many of the water beetles that dive beneath the surface carry a supply of air beneath their hard wing covers. This air is breathed while they are beneath the surface of the water.

Look for water boatmen, dark colored insects about ½ inch in length, having two oar-like appendages which they use to scull themselves through the water. Watch for the giant waterbug, about 1 inch in diameter.

WHAT ON EARTH

Make use of a small household strainer to collect other water life. Some of this will be small insects on which fish feed. Among these are the small wrigglers of the mosquito larvae usually found only in still water. They are called wrigglers from the odd jerking movements with which they reach the surface of the water where they breathe through tubes in their tails.

Look very closely at what you may have caught in the strainer. Some insects are so small and transparent that you will only see them when they move. Among these are the tiny fresh-water shrimp less than ⅛ inch long, and the even smaller cyclops which seems to have but one large eye.

Moving along the bottom of the stream beneath the stones are the larvae of mayflies. With their long hair-tails they crawl from the water onto a stone or stem in late spring or early summer, shedding their old skins and drying out the wings that they have been developing. At this time they dance in clusters above the water and are one of the favorite foods of trout.

On the surface of the water you are apt to see water striders (not spiders). They have comparatively long legs and the weight of each foot makes a tiny dimple in the water as they dart about. They can walk on the water because their weight is spread out and is not sufficient to break the surface tension of the water. They move so fast they are most difficult to capture.

You may also find dark-colored whirligig beetles spinning in circles on the surface of the water. They are ¼ - ½ inch long and move in crazy patterns.

Under rocks in the stream you are certain to find crayfish which look somewhat like small lobsters and are often called crabs. They swim backwards using jerky movements of their tails which curl under them to provide motion. These crayfish are favorite food for bass and raccoons. We often find the legs and claws of crayfish on rocks near a stream where a raccoon has caught and eaten crayfish during the night.

Watch for newts and salamanders along the edges of the stream and in the water beneath stones and rocks. The little orange-red newt often found in damp woodlands is one of the more interesting varieties of salamanders. Part of its life is spent in the water during which time it assumes a dark olive-green color. These small newts are sometimes called red efts.

Newts and other salamanders lay their eggs in masses or ropes of jelly-like transparent material. The tiny dark spots inside are the young salamanders waiting to hatch out. The egg masses are found attached to the under sides of stones and submerged branches.

You will find two colors of tadpoles or pollywogs. Some of these are young frogs and the others are young toads. If they are black they will grow up to be toads. The lighter colored ones will become frogs.

Near the stream you are certain to see dragon flies or darning needles as they are sometimes called. There is no truth in the old story that they can sew up your ears for they are harmless to humans. They are actually dragons to mosquitoes and gnats for both the adults and the young nymphs are swift and deadly when going after their prey. The nymphs move about in the water with their own jet-propulsion system, ejecting water in quick squirts to move themselves along the bottom of the stream. On occasion they have been known to attack and devour tiny fish and tadpoles.

CAMP COOKING GADGETS YOU CAN MAKE

A Charcoal Stove

Obtain a square five gallon can, remove one half of each end leaving a section across two opposite corners as ends for the stove. Use good tin shears for cutting.

With a 2" X 4" and hammer, bend the can into the shape of the letter M having short legs and a wide center as illustrated.

Using an electric drill or spike, make a series of 40 to 50 holes on each of the flat sides for drafts.

Place charcoal in the stove and a grill from an old refrigerator across the top. (Such grills may be obtained at any junkyard or refrigerator dealer. They often may be found in old electric stoves as well.)

A Pot From a No. 10 Can

No. 10 tin cans are often used in outdoor cooking. Improve yours with a handle made from heavy wire such as a coat hanger attached with rivets or small bolts.

Using pliers make an eye in each end of the handle, small enough so that the eyes will not slip over the head of the bolts used for fastening. These should be two small ½" long bolts with two nuts for each. Drill or punch holes at opposite sides of the top of the can, place the bolts through the eyes in the handles, put on a nut then place the bolts through the holes in the tin can and add a second nut. Screw both nuts tightly against the can, leaving the handle loose enough to turn easily.

A Roaster

Obtain a 2 gallon oil can. Remove the handle and mark lines to be cut following the illustration. Cut on the line up the side of the front panel of the can, starting the cut with a cold chisel and finishing with tin-shears. Cut the front free from the top and bottom of the can and bend it outward to serve as reflecting wings. Drill a ¼ inch hole in the center of the top and make a heavy wire skewer with a twisted handle to go through this hole and extending to the bottom of the roaster where the skewer is bent into a flat shape resting on the bottom of the roaster. Meat to be roasted is wrapped around the skewer and wired tightly to hold it in place.

Place the roaster with the meat in front of a reflector fire. Salt the meat well and turn it occasionally until done.

A Reflector Charcoal Fireplace

Obtain a large metal cake tin and remove one end. Cut a piece of chicken wire slightly larger than the front of the tin and fasten the cut wire to the sides and bottom of the tin by punching small holes and twisting the wires tightly through these holes.

Using a heavy wire or other metal support, make a standard to hold the fireplace in an upright position.

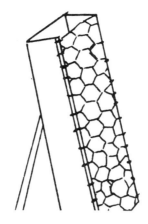

Place charcoal in this fireplace, ignite it, and use it with the above described roaster, or with a reflector oven for baking biscuits, cakes, and pies.

UNEDIBLE (Dangerous) PLANTS

   Children and many adults will eat, or at least chew on, many plants and shrubs which they find in yards, fields, and woods. Many of these plants are harmless and may even be rich in vitamins, but there are others which are definitely dangerous. Even the normally harmless varieties may be contaminated with insecticides or weed killers.

Some of those with which one should become familiar and should avoid because of their dangerous characteristics are:

Chinaberry	Euphorbia	Juniper
Chrysanthemums	Flax	Laburnum
Clematis	Golden Seal	Lady's Slipper
Cohosh	Grape Hyacinth	Larkspur
Columbine	Henbane	Leatherwood
Corn Cockle	Holly Berries	Loco Weed
Cowbane or Water Hemlock	Horsenettle	Locust
Croton	Hyacinth	Maidenhair
Cyclamen	Indian Poke or White Hellebore	Narcissus
Daffodils		Nightshade
Delphinium	Indian Tobacco	Phraxinella
Derris	Jack in the Pulpit	Poison Ivy
Dogwood	Japonica	Poison Oak
Dutchmens' Breeches	Jasmine	Poison Sumac
Elephant Ears	Jimson Weed	White Cedar
	Jonquils	

ADVENTURE IN A TIDE POOL

Adventure is where you find it. Since nearly 75 percent of all life is found in the water, look for a new adventure in the miniature zoos found in the pools left by the receding tides. These are the small ponds where rocks have trapped the waters and the life found in these waters as the tide receded.

The tide pool often contains hundreds of wonderful plants and animals. There may be hermit crabs, crabs that carry seaweed on their backs for camouflage, sea urchins, tiny fish, snails and other creatures bearing shells, and many varieties of seaweed.

Learn where the tide pools are located and plan your trip in advance. You will need a tide table (usually found in the daily newspaper) to know when the tide will be out, for the time of the tide varies from day to day. Wear swim trunks and canvas shoes to protect your feet from sharp rocks and shells, and take along a few heavy plastic bags in which to place sea water to hold your collection.

Once every four weeks, there is an especially high tide followed by a tide lower than normal. It is at the time of this very low tide that the most abundant life is found in the tide pools.

At the tide pool you will learn that every bit of life depends on its own special environment for survival. Some of the life left stranded on the beach or in the tide pool can live for only a few hours outside the sea environment and will soon die if taken away. Don't plan to take your collection of living creatures home, but study them where they are found. Other souvenirs are yours for the taking. These include the thousands of shells that are washed up every day. There may be dead sea urchins looking like small lavender-colored pumpkins. There should be conch shells, snail shells, cowrie shells, spiral shells, mussel and scallop shells, and shells of oysters, razor clams, quahogs and little-neck clams, barnacles, limpets, and many others.

Make the Most of Nature

Examine kelp and seaweed for the shellfish that attach themselves to these plants. Try tying a piece of mussel on a string and dangle it close to openings in the rocks to see if you can entice rock crabs from their hiding places.

And when your trip is about to end, return all living creatures to the place where they were found.

If you should find a starfish, take it home to your aquarium. The starfish, which is actually not a fish at all, is shaped like a five-pointed star and, when full grown, may be six inches across and about one inch thick at the center. It is brown in color and is covered with many small plates and points. On the lower side are furrows extending from each of the five arms towards the center where the opening of the mouth has five teeth which meet in the center. From rows of tiny holes in each of the furrows protrude slender tubes ending in suction discs which the starfish uses to move across the ocean floor.

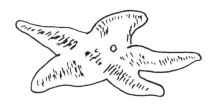

Starfish are found in many sizes and shapes. Some are short and fat, others long and snaky. On some the arms have many branches. When a starfish loses an arm it grows another, and when cut in half, each half will grow into a separate starfish.

Starfish do a tremendous amount of damage, especially to oyster beds where they attach their suction cups to the oyster shells, pulling until the oyster is exhausted and the shell opens, whereupon the starfish eats the oyster.

WHAT ON EARTH

Sea urchins, sometimes called the "little hedgehogs of the sea", have prickly coats of spines like a hedgehog. They are found in a variety of shapes. Some are pumpkin-shaped and other flat like sand dollars. On the underside there is a five-pointed arrangement of tubes and suction discs like the starfish.

With their bristly coats, the smaller spherical sea urchins resemble chestnut burrs. The larger varieties may have thumb-and-finger-shaped appendages among their spines with which they pick out any debris that becomes entangled in their bristly coats. They feed on the mud of the sea bottom from which their stomachs extract the minute bits of food found there.

The shells which you may find are the homes which mol-lusks and some other animals build for themselves from substances, mainly carbonate of lime, secreted from their glands.

As a mollusk grows, the shell increases in size and thick-ness. Growth is indicated by the ridges that run parallel with the outer edge of the shell. Points and other protuberances on the shell result from similar projections of muscular tissue on the back of the mollusk. The shell is made up of three layers. The outer layer contains no lime and is formed of a hornlike material. Beneath this is a layer of carbonate of lime and then an inner layer of mother-of-pearl which is tran-lucent and shows beautiful colors due to its ability to refract the light.

Most shells fit into two groups known as univalves and bi-valves. The univalves are in one piece like those of the snail. The bivalves are in two parts like those of the oyster and clam. A smaller third class, called the chitons, consists of eight overlapping plates sometimes called "coat-of-mail" shells.

Most univalve shells are conical with a spiral turning coun-ter-clockwise when seen from above. Occasional left-handed shells are found twisting in the opposite direction.

Certain shells were once used as money by primitive peoples. These included the wampum of the American Indian made from cylindrical pieces of quahog, periwinkle, and welk shells, rubbed until smooth and strung like beads. The purple wampus made from the quahog shells had the highest value.

If you wish to add the shells you find to your collection, live animals may be removed from the shells by dipping them in boiling water for a couple of minutes and then removing the body with tweezers. If the shells are too small to permit removal in this manner, soak them in a seventy percent alcohol solution for at least 24 hours and then allow them to dry in the shade.

Larger bivalves may be placed in boiling water until the shells open. Remove the body of the mollusk and then tie the shell shut with string until the hinge dries out. The string may then be removed and the shell will remain closed.

Shell collections should be labeled correctly with notes showing where and under what conditions they were found. Books that may be useful for identification of shells include the following:

Introducing Seashells; a Colorful Guide for the Beginning Collector. By Robert T. Abbott (Van Nostrand 1955)
First Book of Sea Shells. By Betty Cavanna (Watts 1955)

The crab is closely related to the shrimp, lobster, and crayfish. Its shell is jointed and is called a carapace. It has five pairs of walking legs including the larger pincers. In swimming crabs, the last pair of legs is flattened for swimming. Attached to the abdomen are from one to four pairs of small legs called swimmerets. The eggs of the female are often found attached to these swimmerets.

The eyes of the crab are mounted on two stalks which can be drawn back inside the shell or carapace. There are also two pairs of antennae. One pair is long and single-stalked; the other pair is short and branches into two parts.

The abdomen of the crab is carried folded forward under the larger part of the crab's body which is called the cephalo-thorax. Crabs breathe by means of gills if they live in the water or organs similar to lungs if they live on the land.

The crabs, found in the tide pools, are apt to be fiddlers, rock, sand or stone crabs which live on the shore near the water and dig into the sand. The fiddler crab gets its name from its one large claw on its right front leg. As the crab moves about, it brandishes this claw in a back and forth motion somewhat like a violinist moves his fiddle. It burrows backwards into the sand and uses the large claw to open and close the burrow and also as a means of defense.

The hermit crab has a long, soft abdomen which it thrusts into an empty shell holding itself in place with hook-like organs on its abdomen. As the crab moves about it drags the shell behind it. As the crab grows, it may move into a larger shell. Sometimes a second sea animal will attach itself to the open end of the same shell building up and enlarging the open end of the shell and living in cooperation with the hermit crab, sharing the same food supply

The tiny pea crab lives inside the shell of an oyster or mussel and helps to destroy the organisms that might injure its host. Some crabs cover themselves with living pieces of seaweed or sponge as a disguise.

Most crabs are scavengers, living on dead and decaying material. A few feed on living vegetation and small animals.

Crabs go through several stages of metamorphosis, shedding their shells by pulling their bodies through a narrow crack in the upper shell. In the first stages of metamorphosis, the young crab larvae look totally unlike a crab, being long and spiny, with enormous eyes and fringed antennae and very large mouthparts which are used for swimming.

Somewhere between the coasts of North America and Africa there is an immense mass of seaweed nearly as large as a continent, perhaps first discovered by Columbus. This mass is the home of many fish and other deep-sea creatures. The seaweed in this mass is a free-floating variety. Close to the shore we find seaweed attached to rocks except when torn loose by wave action. The seaweed we find in a tide pool may be green, brown, red, or blue-green. The giant kelps are the largest and may grow into tough leathery streamers 150 feet in length.

Seaweeds help to keep sea water pure by giving off oxygen. They are used as fertilizers and in the manufacture of glass, soap, and iodine. Some seaweeds contain gelatin and are edible. These may be used to make seaweed pudding. They are also sometimes used as cattle feed and a large amount of seaweed is used for stuffing mattresses and furniture.

SAND MODELING

Playing in the sand is an appealing activity to boys and girls from the youngest one in a sandbox to more mature young people at the seashore.

A good knowledge of just how to model sand adds real interest.

The best sand for modeling is very fine, sharp, unwashed river sand or the fine, white sand of the seashore. A very small amount of soil mixed with the sand aids in holding its shape while modeling.

The sand should be thoroughly sifted while dry through a fine sieve and then moistened at least an hour before using so that the water will disperse evenly throughout the sand. At the proper consistency, the sand will hold together when squeezed in the hand, retaining the imprints of the fingers.

There are three basic methods of modeling sand:

Modeling in the Round—Pile up sand following the general outline of the figure to be sculptured and then fill in the details.

Flat Modeling—Start with a level area of sand and fill in with wet sand to bring details into relief.

Bas-Relief Modeling—Modeling sand is piled in a pyramid with an approximate 45 degree slope to the side. Sketch the outline to be modeled on the side of the pyramid and then build up with wet sand or cut away sand to bring out the design.

Tools Needed:

The best tools are the hands for shaping, adding, and removing sand. Other tools may be two flat boards, one used in each hand to push sand into general shapes and to press it into a smooth, solid form; flat-bottomed potato-masher-shaped pieces of wood for tamping surfaces; pointed sticks for fine detail; and thin sharp-edged pieces of wood for slicing away unwanted sand and for shaping.

Preserving Models:

The addition of salt, molasses or glue to the water used for mixing will help keep the models from crumbling. To keep models for a number of days, sprinkle them while moist with a thin coat of dry cement.

Color may be added by sprinkling the moist models with dry poster (Tempera) paints, or liquid paints or dyes may be sprayed on the models.

SAND CASTING

Damp sand has the unusual ability to make very accurate impressions and is easy to handle as well. It has been used since ancient times for the molding of cast iron objects and is most adaptable for the molding of nature items to be cast in plaster of Paris.

You can press almost anything you wish into damp sand, leaving a fine print for casting. Try such things as fossils, leaves, shells, fish, seed pods, etc.

Materials needed are:

> Plaster of Paris or Molding Plaster which is available at most lumber and building supply dealers and is much cheaper than plaster of Paris.

> Small wooden boxes to hold sand. The boxes should be 2 inches to 3 inches deep. Why not make them?

> Sand—preferably fine, sifted sand. Ordinary sand sifted through window screening will work but the finer it is, the better.

> Plastic mixing bowl

> Sprinkling bottle (laundry type)

> Old tablespoon or wooden spoon

> Water

> Pieces of copper wire 3 to 4 inches long, twisted into a loop for hanging, leaving tails at least 1 inch long to imbed in plaster.

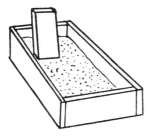

Firm and smooth the moist sand with a wooden block before pressing in the objects to be molded.

Sift sand and place in wooden box. Add small amounts of water from the sprinkling bottle until the sand is firm enough to hold its shape and to keep any impressions made in it. Firm the sand using a small flat piece of wood. Keep the top surface of the sand perfectly level and smooth.

Press the objects to be molded into the sand. Do this carefully to leave a good impression of the article to be cast. Remove the objects carefully so as not to disturb the sand at the edges of the impressions.

Mix plaster and water quickly and carefully. Add water to the plaster in your plastic mixing bowl, stirring constantly until there are no lumps remaining and the mixture is the consistency of heavy cream. Lumps are apt to remain in the bottom of the bowl so be sure to mix well.

As soon as the plaster is well mixed, pour it into the mold until it reaches a depth of ¾ to 1 inch.

Twist a 3 to 4 inch piece of copper wire into a loop having long ends. Place this wire hanger in the plaster at the top of the mold with the long ends extending into the plaster at an angle. The loop of the wire should extend about ½ inch from the plaster and will hang the finished casting.

As soon as the plaster has been poured, wash the plastic bowl and mixing-spoon before the plaster dries. Never mix more plaster in a container in which there is plaster from a former mix or the new mix will not harden properly.

Leave the plaster casting in place overnight to harden. Remove it from the mold by taking the wooden box apart. Place the casting in a warm, dry place to cure. It will take from 3 days to a week to become completely dry. Brush all loose sand from the casting.

The finished cast may be painted using water colors, airplane dope, or tempera colors, or the parts of the cast may be stained using regular wood stains.

MEASURING WITHOUT A RULE

Distances across a stream or ravine, the height of a tree or building, and other distances can be measured fairly accurately without a rule or tape when you have a little knowledge of and experience in how it is done.

There are certain dimensions that you always carry with you and which can be used more or less as a ruler.

1. Length of step

2. Height

3. Distance from finger tip to finger tip when both arms are spread.

4. Height of eyes from the ground

5. Length of forearm, fingertip to elbow

6. Span of hand, tip of thumb to tip of little finger when all fingers are spread.

7. Breadth of thumb

8. Length of forefinger

Learn the length of your average step. Measure off a 100 foot course and walk this course several times using your normal step. Count the number of steps for each 100 feet and figure the average number of steps per 100 feet. Divide this average into 100 feet and you will have the length of your average step. Forty steps would be 2½ feet per step. Fifty steps would be 2 feet per step, etc. With this knowledge you can measure other distances. Walk along the distance to be measured, counting the number of steps. Multiply the number of steps by the average length of your step and you will be close to the correct distance.

Suppose the distance to be measured is across a river or ravine where you cannot walk. Here is what you do in that case.

Hold a stick 2 to 3 feet long in your outstretched hand, keeping the arm level with the ground. Lower the stick until

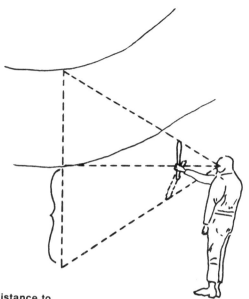

Pace off this distance to get stream width.

the line of sight touches both the top of the stick and the opposite bank of the stream or ravine.

Without moving the stick, slide the hand up or down the stick until the line of sight from the eye past the thumb, touches the near bank of the stream, or ravine.

Now without changing the elevation of the arm or stick, turn to the stream or ravine and again look over the top of the stick and along the position of the thumb. Mentally mark the spots where the line of sight touches on each sighting. Lower the stick and pace off the distances between these two points, counting each step. Multiply the number of steps by the length of your step and you will have the approximate distance across the stream or ravine.

WHAT ON EARTH

Suppose the distance to be measured is the height of a tree or building. Holding a 2 to 3 foot stick upright in your outstretched hand, step back a convenient distance from the tree or building. Again sight across the top of the stick at the top of the tree and move the hand holding the stick until a sighting along the thumb touches the bottom of the tree. Without moving from the spot and without lowering the arm, turn the stick downward 90 degrees or level with the ground.

With the line of sight across the thumb still touching the bottom of the tree or building, sight across the end of the stick and mentally mark the spot where the line of sight touches the ground. Pace off the distance from this spot to the base of the tree, counting the number of steps and multiplying this number by the average length of your step. This will give you the approximate height in feet of the tree or building.

Pace off this distance to get tree height.

TRAIL MARKERS THAT REFLECT THE LIGHT

Trails are easier to follow in sun, shadow, and darkness when they are marked with reflective tape which may be purchased at hardware and auto supply stores. Colors may be either red or silver and may be used alone or in combination in a variety of patterns to indicate the specific trail being followed.

Masonite, cut to the desired shape, makes an excellent background with the reflective tape being applied in a definite design as suggested in the accompanying illustrations.

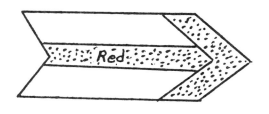

MAKING PEMMICAN—the INDIAN FOOD

Pemmican was a nutritive food made by the Indians; a food that would keep for a long time, and one that was often the only food carried on long trips when weight was important.

A modern form of pemmican can be made from easily available foods and used on long hikes and camping trips.

You will need approximately equal amounts of the following ingredients:

Chipped beef
Shelled pecans
Raisins
Suet

Place the chipped beef on a drying board in the open air and allow it to dry until crisp. Grind the dried chipped beef, the pecans, and the raisins in separate containers.

Render the fat from the suet over a low heat and when melted, strain well to remove any pieces that have not melted.

Mix equal parts of the three ground ingredients and then add just enough of the melted suet to hold it together. It will take only a small amount.

Line a flat cake pan with aluminum foil and place the mixture in this while it is still soft. Spread the mixture evenly about ¾ inches thick and allow to cool.

When cool, cut the pemmican into pieces the size of a candy bar and wrap each piece in foil. It will keep for a long time and is a fine food for camping and hiking.

MAKING A NOGGIN

A noggin is a pioneer drinking cup carved from a tree burl, one of those odd-shaped bumps that often grow on the sides of trees.

Select a burl somewhat larger than you wish the finished cup to be, and before cutting it from the tree, peel off the outside bark to see if it is decayed or has a hole in it.

When a good burl has been selected, saw it from the tree making sure to leave an extended piece of wood to be carved into a small handle. Paint the wound on the tree with a preservative paint to prevent rot.

Bore several holes in the flat surface where the burl was sawed from the tree. Using a sharp knife, carefully carve out the inside of the burl using care not to cut a hole through the noggin.

Carve the sides of the cup fairly thin but not thin enough so that it will crack or break easily. Sand both the inside and the outside to get them smooth. Carve out a handle and then drill a hole through which tie a leather thong for carrying. When finished, soak the noggin in linseed oil for about 24 hours. Wipe it dry and polish it with a soft rag.

Melt some beeswax in a tin can and mix in enough turpentine to make a thick paste. Keep the turpentine away from the fire to prevent accidents.

Rub the beeswax paste into the outside of the cup and polish it well. This will make a beautiful and durable finish that only hot water can destroy. Attach a leather thong to the handle with a large knot and add a toggle or wooden knob at the other end of the thong leaving the thong about one foot long. This is for tying to the belt on a hike or hunting trip.

HERPETOLOGY
The Study of Reptiles and Amphibians

Herpetology can be fun, especially for boys. Before going out on a collecting expedition, build a number of cages in which snakes and other amphibians may be kept for a short time.

Cages may be simple but must be well built for a snake can get through an opening that most persons would not even notice. Build snake cages about the length of the snake and about one half as wide and high. Cages for amphibians such as frogs, salamanders, lizards, etc. need to be large enough for the animals to move around freely.

Go on a collecting hike on a warm day keeping a sharp lookout for movement on the ground. Snakes are often found near barns, in rock piles, under logs and stones, or near water. Frogs and salamanders are found along stream banks, in wet spots, and under rotten logs. On warm days they are often found sunning themselves on warm rocks.

The best way to collect these animals is in carrying bags which can be tied at the top. Small cloth bags are excellent. Do not collect snakes and other amphibians in the same bag.

WHAT ON EARTH

Snakes prefer live food such as mice, frogs, rats, birds, and eggs. Sometimes they will eat other snakes and fish.

Salamanders and lizards live on insects such as flies, grubs, and termites.

There are only four kinds of dangerous snakes in the United States. They are rattlesnakes, copperheads, water moccasins, and coral snakes. These should not be collected except by experts. Other snakes are relatively harmless and may be safely collected. You will find that they are generally good-natured, clean animals that are easy to raise and tame.

When collecting and raising becomes a hobby, start keeping records such as:

1. Variety, date, and place collected
2. Their measurements
3. What they eat
4. When they shed their skins and how they do it
5. When eggs are laid and young are born
6. When they become sick and die
7. Their scientific names
8. What they do that may be either good or harmful

These records will help you to learn more about them.

RECOGNIZING SOARING HAWKS

Hawks, eagles, osprey, and vultures are often seen soaring at great heights where they can be identified only by the shapes of their silhouettes against the sky. Each has its own shape and with practice can be identified with comparative ease. Learn to recognize their individual shapes from the following illustrations.

BALD EAGLE
GOLDEN EAGLE
OSPREY } all have long, wide wings and a short tail.
TURKEY VULTURE
BLACK VULTURE

BALD EAGLE

OSPREY

MARSH HAWK } has long, wide wings and a long tail.

MARSH HAWK

RED-SHOULDERED HAWK
RED-TAILED HAWK } have wide wings and a fan-shaped tail.
BROAD-WINGED HAWK

RED-SHOULDERED HAWK

COOPER'S HAWK

COOPER'S HAWK
SHARP-SHINNED HAWK } have short wings and long tails.
GOSHAWK

SHARP-SHINNED HAWK

The FALCONS
DUCK HAWK } have pointed wings and long tails.
SPARROW HAWK

DUCK HAWK

SPARROW HAWK

INSECT-EATING PLANTS

Plants provide food for millions of insects which suck their juices and feed on their roots and leaves. Once in a while, however, we come upon plants that eat insects instead. These plants are very interesting and are not as hard to find as one might suppose. Most of these plants are hidden away in deep swamps. It is all in knowing where to look for them.

There are three distinct groups of plants that trap and eat insects. These are the Pitcher Plants, the Sundews, and the Venus Flytrap. Their food is nitrogen which they get from their victims.

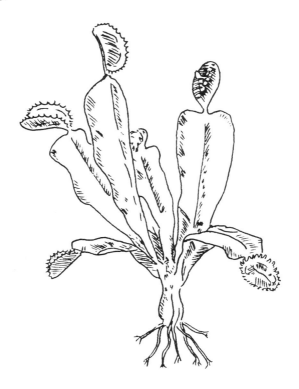

Pitcher plants are found in open areas for they need plenty of light for growth. They have yellow or purple flowers which attract insects but it is the unusual trap-shaped leaves which do the work. Near the edge of their leaves is found a perfume which draws the insects. When an unsuspecting insect alights on one of these leaves, the leaf closes with an interlocking set of teeth on each edge of the leaf preventing the insect's escape. Juices inside the leaves slowly digest the insect. When digestion is complete, the leaf opens to await its next victim.

Sundews may be found in wet, spongy places almost anywhere in the United States. The upper surfaces of the leaves of these plants are covered with long hairs having swollen tips covered with a sticky fluid which attracts insects. Insects touching these hairs, make them fold inwards trapping the insect. The hairs do not unfold until digestion is complete.

The Venus Flytrap is found in the low sandy bogs and pine lands of the southeast. The leaves are flat and blade-like, having snares at their tips. These snares are hinged down the middle with each half having a fringe of long bristles. The surfaces are covered with hairs which, when touched, cause the traps to snap shut making a prison for any insect caught. The insect is actually kept a prisoner until food is needed by the plant when it will proceed to digest it.

A NATURE STAKEOUT

A nature stakeout may be done by individuals or by several persons in a group.

Drive four wooden pegs into the ground to form a square about 1 ft. on each side. Lie on your stomach and make a careful examination of your square foot of earth. What do you see? What different kinds of plants are there? What do you know about them?

Do you see anything alive? See how many different kinds of living creatures you can find. How many signs are there that something alive has been there? Are there holes in which insects or worms live? Have any living things left droppings there? Are there webs of any kind? Have insects or animals been feeding on the vegetation there or on each other?

What kinds of pebbles are there in your stakeout?

Make a list of all the things you see.

At the end of an agreed upon time, check your list with others taking part in the stakeout.

Try a stakeout again in a different kind of location. It might be in the fields, in the woods, on a lawn, along a stream bank, on a beach, in a desert, or on rocks.

You will find that there are a great many things happening in this miniature world that you never suspected. After a few stakeouts you will find that you are seeing many things that you never saw before.

ADVENTURES IN WEATHER FORECASTING

What is it that makes weather? Where does it come from? How can we know what the weather may be like tomorrow? Is it going to rain or will the sun shine?

The weather affects what we do, probably more than any one other thing. It affects the way we feel and act; it affects the places we go; it even affects the way we travel and the way we live. Stores, sports, farming, travel, recreation, and vacations are all so affected by the weather that we have set up methods for making and reporting weather forecasts from one day to several days in advance. In fact it is now possible to make weather predictions with some accuracy several months in advance.

Weather forecasting is done by using data sent in regularly from points all over the country and now includes reports from weather satellites orbiting around the earth.

The weather forecaster depends on certain implements or "tools" which are affected by temperature, pressure, and humidity. We can make our own simple instruments and forecast the weather with a reasonable degree of accuracy. From the data of these homemade instruments we can also record the wind direction and velocity, the rainfall, and the cloud cover.

By keeping accurate listings of these types of data we will soon discover that a certain kind of weather normally follows certain conditions which we have measured. Check your own forecasts with those of the local weather bureau as reported on radio, television, or in the newspapers. Occasionally, both you and the regular weather forecasters may be wrong, but you will find yourself becoming more and more accurate as your experience increases.

Building a Wind Gauge *(anemometer)*

A wind gauge is called an anemometer.

Glue two flat sticks ¾ inch in thickness and 18 inches long at right angles at their centers. When the glue is dry, drill a

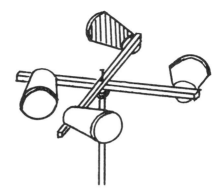

small hole at the exact center of the point where the two sticks cross. This hole should be just a slight bit larger than a nail which is to be driven through the hole into the end of a length of heavy doweling or broomstick which is about 2 feet long. Before driving the nail into the dowel, place two small washers over the nail so that it will come between the cross sticks and the dowel enabling the anemometer to turn easily. A large, round, wooden bead may work even better than the washers. The bead should be between ¼ and ½ inch in diameter.

Staple four paper cups to the cross arms, one at the end of each arm with all cups opening in the same direction. Color one of the paper cups to make it easier to count the number of revolutions of the anemometer as it is turned by the wind.

Fasten the dowel part of the anemometer upright in an open area where the wind has a clean sweep and can turn the anemometer as it passes.

To calculate the speed of the wind, count the number of turns of the colored paper cup for 30 seconds. Divide this number by five to get the approximate speed of the wind in miles per hour.

Measuring the Relative Humidity

The relative humidity of the air is measured by a wet-dry thermometer called a hygrometer.

Two thermometers are mounted on a board having a small shelf beneath the thermometers. Place a piece of lamp-wicking over the bulb of one of the thermometers and let the wicking hang into a cup or tin can of water setting on the shelf.

To get the correct relative humidity, read both of the thermometers. Subtract the lower from the higher reading to get the difference. From the following chart, read the relative humidity.

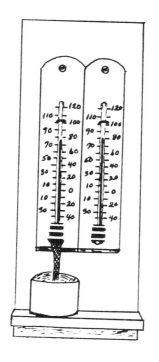

Measuring Air Pressure *(Make an Aneroid Barometer)*

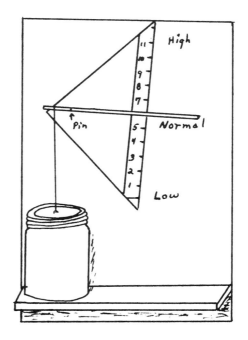

Obtain a glass fruit jar having a metal screw top with a removable inner part. Using only the screw top with the inner part removed, place a sheet of thin plastic over the top of the jar and screw the top in place to hold the plastic securely.

Glue a piece of thread to the center of the plastic and glue or tie the opposite end to one end of a soda straw. One inch from the end of the straw where the thread is fastened, run a straight pin through the straw and into a supporting board. Beneath the opposite end of the straw, place a cardboard measure marked off in inches like a ruler. Place this measure so that when the straw is in a horizontal position it will rest over the middle figure of the ruler. (See illustration). Mark this position "Normal". Mark the lower end of the ruler "Low" and the upper end "High".

As the air pressure changes, the plastic diaphragm will move up or down with the end of the straw moving to indicate the relative change in air pressure. Changes to higher pressures are indications that good weather is coming. Changes to lower pressure indicate the weather will be changing for the worse.

Make a Simple Bottle Barometer

Barometers are used to forecast weather. They actually measure the air pressure and since the air pressure changes somewhat in advance of changes in the weather a barometer can be used to forecast such changes.

Obtain a glass milk bottle and a smaller bottle the neck of which will extend into the milk bottle and which will fit snugly into the top of the milk bottle.

WHAT ON EARTH

Fill the milk bottle with water to a point about 1 inch above the mouth of the inverted smaller bottle when placed inside. Now remove the smaller bottle and fill it about half full with water, placing it upside down inside the top of the milk bottle. With a felt marker or piece of adhesive tape, mark the level of the water in the smaller bottle.

Changes in the air pressure will cause the level of water in the smaller bottle to rise or fall. An increase in air-pressure, meaning that better weather is coming, will cause the water-level to rise. Decreasing air pressure, meaning poorer weather, will cause the water-level to lower.

Use these changes in air-pressure to forecast changes in the weather within a few hours.

Measuring Precipitation

Obtain any slender straight-sided glass or plastic container such as a test-tube, toothbrush container, etc. If the bottom of the container is not flat on the inside, tap a little modeling clay in the bottom to make it level.

Fasten the tube to an upright board and tack a small ruler alongside with the lower end of the ruler even with the inside bottom of the tube. Place this rain-gauge in the open where it will receive direct rainfall.

The amount of precipitation each day should be read from the ruler and recorded in a notebook or on your weather record along with other informa-
tion on the weather for the day. After each reading, empty the water from the tube so that the next reading will be accurate. Do not use the gauge during freez-ing weather for ice will crack the tube.

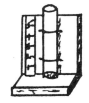

Keeping a Weather Record

Keep an accurate weather record from each of your home-made instruments and your visual observations. It could look something like this:

MY WEATHER RECORD
Year - 1969

Date	Barometer	Relative Humidity	Precipitation	Time and Temperature	Winds	Sky	My Forecast (for tomorrow)	Weatherman's Forecast (for tomorrow)	Actual Weather
March 1	Falling		½ inch	4:00 P.M. 30 degrees	Westerly 5 mph.	Cloudy	Snow, colder	Clear, colder	Clear, colder
March 2	Steady		None	4:00 P.M. 22 degrees	None	Clear	Clear, warmer	Cloudy, warmer	Partly cloudy, warmer
March 3	Rising		None	4:00 P.M. 29 degrees	Northerly 7 mph.	Partly cloudy	Clear, cold	Clear, cold, windy	Clear, cold, gusty
March 4	Rising		None	3:30 P.M. 15 degrees	Northerly 15 mph.	Clear	Clear, cold	Cloudy, warmer	Cloudy, warmer
March 5	Falling		None	5:00 P.M. 32 degrees	Southerly 2 mph.	Cloudy	Snow, warmer	Snow, warmer	Snow, warmer
March 6									

Relative Humidity Table

The percent of humidity in the air can be taken from this table. Subtract the reading of the wet-bulb thermometer from that of the dry-bulb thermometer, finding the difference between the two. Read across the top line of the chart to locate the column beneath the figure indicating this difference. Follow down this column to the number opposite the reading on the dry-bulb thermometer. This number is the relative humidity or percent of humidity in the air.

Example: The reading of the wet-bulb thermometer is 64 and of the dry-bulb thermometer 70. The difference is 6. Beneath the number 6 on the top line of the chart we follow down to the number opposite the reading 70 of the dry-bulb thermometer. This number is 72 and is the relative humidity.

	1°	2°	3°	4°	6°	8°	10°	12°	14°	16°	18°	20°	22°
0°	82	50	32	16									
10°	85	60	45	32	5								
20°	88	70	56	46	24	5							
30°	90	79	68	58	38	18	8						
40°	92	84	76	68	52	37	22	10					
50°	93	87	80	74	61	49	37	26	16	5			
60°	94	89	84	78	68	58	43	39	30	21	13	5	
70°	95	90	86	81	72	64	55	48	40	33	26	19	11
80°	96	92	87	83	75	63	61	54	47	41	35	29	23
90°	96	93	88	85	78	71	65	54	52	47	41	36	32
100°	97	93	90	86	80	74	68	62	57	51	47	42	37
110°	98	94	91	87	81	76	71	64	60	56	51	46	41

MAKING AND THROWING A BOOMERANG

One of the most fascinating of nature craft projects is the successful making and throwing of a boomerang. Thousands of years ago primitive peoples in many parts of the world discovered that they could make carefully shaped sticks that would curve in flight and that might be used for hunting, for war, and for their own amusement. Some of these were so designed that they would return to the thrower. This type was used principally for sport and amusement.

It was the Aborigines of Australia who developed the boomerang as we know it, a two-armed U-shaped stick, two to four feet in length, flat on one side and rounded on the other and having one sharp and one dull edge.

The motion of the boomerang is caused by the action of the air on the rounded side. There is no magic in this action for it works on the well known aerodynamic principle of "lift".

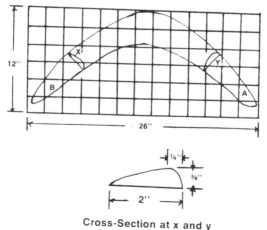

Cross-Section at x and y

Note: *The above directions are for making a boomerang for right-handed persons. The left-handed thrower should fashion his boomerang flat on the opposite side to the right-handed boomerang.*

WHAT ON EARTH

The underside of the boomerang is nearly flat and the upper side rounded, being thicker at the leading edge and thinner at the following edge. This means that one arm of the boomerang is thicker on the outside edge and the other arm thicker on the inside edge for these are the forward or leading edges as the boomerang rotates and travels.

A cross section of each arm is in the shape of an elongated teardrop. The length of the arms is important only in that the boomerang with the longer arms can be thrown for a greater distance. Arms lengths may vary but both arms are the same in any one boomerang. The thickest part of the arms should be between ¼ and ⅜ inches.

Following the illustrations, draw and cut out a paper pattern, tracing the pattern on any tough hardwood such as maple, hickory, ash, etc., preferably starting with wood about ½ inch thick.

Saw the wood to the shape of the pattern and finish shaping with a wood rasp and sandpaper. Leave the underside flat and shape the arms according to the cross section drawings.

Carefully balance the boomerang by suspending with a string tied at the center. File and sand each arm until perfectly balanced.

The boomerang is not thrown side-arm, but overhand like a baseball. Hold the boomerang by the arm marked B in the illustration. Then as it is thrown the thicker edges of arms A and B will be the leading edges.

In throwing, hold the boomerang in a nearly vertical position with a slight tilt towards the flat side. Throw from a running step, with a snap of the wrist to make the boomerang spin.

Practice throwing to achieve accuracy and to make the boomerang return to your feet. With practice one should be able to make the boomerang travel 75 to 150 feet before returning.

Throwing position.

Remember that the boomerang is a dangerous object. Never throw one when other people, animals, or buildings are within 100 yards of you. And never attempt to catch a returning boomerang for its rotating arms can cause serious injury.

COLLECTING AND POLISHING PEBBLES

Young people are always collecting interesting pebbles found along a stream bed. Add to the fun by grinding and polishing them. There will be color patterns that are much more beautiful when they are polished.

You will need these materials:

Silicon Carbide sandpaper (either wet or dry types)
1 sheet coarse   cut these into quarters and tack one
1 sheet medium   piece of each to a smooth wooden
1 sheet fine   block.

Chamois Skin (a small piece of an old one will do). Chamois Skin is the material often used in drying automobiles after they have been washed. Tack the chamois to a smooth wooden block.

A can of fine grit polishing agent such as "Bon Ami" or a fine pumice.
A pan of water

Select a pebble to be ground and polished. Start with the flattest surface of the pebble.

Grind the stone first on the coarse sandpaper, keeping the paper wet while grinding. A back and forth or circular motion will do. Continue this grinding until the surface is smooth and

Grind on silicon carbide paper.

Coarse   **Medium**   **Fine**

**Polish on wet chamois to which
polishing material has been added**

Wet chamois

without defects. Wash the pebble occasionally so you can see how the grinding is progressing.

When the surface is smooth, change to the medium sandpaper and grind until all of the scratches from the coarse sandpaper have been removed. Wash. Finish the grinding on the fine sandpaper until the entire surface appears to be frosted.

The final job is polishing. Wet the chamois skin and add some of the polishing material. Rub well until the entire surface is shiny.

Be sure each step is completed before starting the next.

SEED MOSAICS

Mosaics, made from a variety of seeds are clever, attractive, and fun to make.

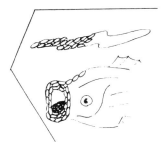

Corn in various colors, colored beans, squash seeds, cucumber and muskmelon seeds, pits from dates, olives, peaches, plums, apple seeds, pepper and tomato seeds, and many other kinds of seeds may be used.

Select or draw a pattern having masses of color without too much detail. Draw this pattern on the background material to be used. A sheet of medium sandpaper makes an interestingly textured background.

Glue the seeds in place, one at a time, filling in with the seeds of the desired color as needed.

Cement the finished mosaic to a piece of thin plywood or masonite and place in a frame.

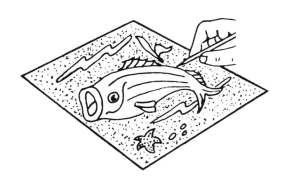

INSECT COLLECTION BOXES

In preparation for making an insect collection, it is wise to make one or more collection-boxes in advance, having them ready for insects as they are collected.

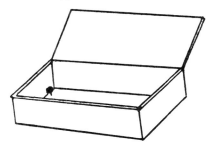

Obtain a few empty cigar boxes, a sheet of styrofoam from ½ to 1 inch thick, white glue, mothballs, a sharp knife, ruler, pencil, straight pins, and a pair of pliers.

Measure the inside dimensions of each cigar box and cut styrofoam pieces to fit. Glue these in place with white cement. (Do not use plastic or model cement for they are apt to dissolve the styrofoam.)

Heat the head of a pin while holding it with the pliers and, while hot, push the head into one of the mothballs to about the center. Two mothballs are needed for each box. They are placed in opposite corners of the box and will prevent tiny insects such as clothes-moth larvae, ants, etc. from destroying your insect collection. Anchor the mothballs in place by pushing the pins into the styrofoam base.

Insects to be mounted are placed on insect pins available from school supply houses and from such places as stores on college campuses.

Complete directions for making an insect collecting net, an insect killing bottle, an insect spreading board, and mounting insects are found in CREATIVE NATURE CRAFTS by R. O. Bale, Burgess Publishing Company, 426 Sixth Street, Minneapolis 15, Minnesota; 1959.

LET'S BUILD A TERRARIUM
Dish Garden

A terrarium is an indoor garden made in a glass container such as a fish bowl, mayonnaise jar, or other glass container of almost any size. Large containers are easier to fill and care for than small ones. The container should have a lid or cover of some kind.

Before constructing a terrarium, decide on the kind you wish to make. It may be from a woodland, a miniature desert, an old field, a seashore, or lake shore.

Materials to be placed in the terrarium should be gathered with this in mind.

Perhaps the easiest is a woodland scene. For this, gather small items which will fit in the container without crowding. Gather such things as small lichens (British soldiers, fairy castles, reindeer moss, and lichens growing on small stones and rotting wood), mosses, tiny evergreen seedlings, small plants such as wintergreen, trailing arbutus, ivy, tiny ferns, tiny vines, etc.; two or three small dry leaves, pieces of rotting wood, acorns, small cones and other woodland specimens. Keep everything in miniature.

Collect enough soil from the woods to fill the container to a depth of about two inches.

Place the collected specimens carefully in the soil, arranging them to give a natural appearance.

The terrarium should be moist but not wet. Unless the soil is extremely dry when it is placed in the container, no additional moisture should be necessary.

When all specimens are in place, cover the terrarium with a lid, piece of glass, or plastic.

Place the terrarium in the light, but not in the direct sun. Regulate the temperature and moisture by opening or closing the top. If moisture condenses on the top and sides, remove the cover until it is clear again, then replace.

Small animals or insects may be added to the terrarium. These might include tiny toads, newts, spiders, snails, salamanders, etc. A few insects will provide food for the animals.

A well-built terrarium will last for several months if the temperature and moisture are carefully controlled. Too much moisture will cause mildew and will kill the plants. Too high a temperature will also kill the plants and animals in the terrarium.

NATURE PICTURES

Nature pictures are carefully arranged and mounted plant materials found in the out-of-doors. The plant materials used are best if they are dried and pressed flat. Flowers should be simple, easily pressed types, rather than heavy, fleshy flowers. Buttercups, Queen Anne's Lace, violets, pansies, etc. are excellent, as are most leaves.

Using a heavy paper backing such as freezer paper or butcher's wrapping paper, arrange the specimens of plant materials, leaves or simple flowers to form a pleasing design. These are to be carefully placed on the paper backing.

Over these specimens, place a single thickness of tissue paper or facial tissue.

Prepare a mixture of ⅓ white glue and ⅔ water. Brush this over the tissue, brushing out all air bubbles and sealing the tissue to the paper backing. When dry, mount the nature pictures on heavy cardboard. They may be framed for hanging.

Japanese rice paper may be used in place of other tissues and adds a pleasing touch to the pictures.

PRESSING AND MOUNTING FLOWERS

This is a fascinating hobby and can result in beautiful wall hangings, placemats, pictures, notepaper, or place cards.

Use flowers that are fresh, with brilliant colors and pleasing designs. Select those having a single thickness of petals so that each petal will show after pressing.

Press the flowers as soon as they are picked to keep their beauty and to make them lie flat. Press until the flowers are completely dry for any dampness remaining will ruin the finished product.

Press between two flat boards covered with newspapers and a single thickness of muslin cloth. Arrange the flowers on the muslin, then cover with a second piece of muslin, more newspapers, and the second board. Use bricks or stones to provide pressure on the top board. (You may prefer to make a press using two pieces of heavy plywood with bolts and winged nuts to provide the pressure, or a book press may be used.)

When pressed well, the flowers will stick to the cloth. Loosen them by grasping the cloth at the corners and stretching it. Keep the dried flowers between the pages of a book or magazine until ready to be used. It will take about three weeks for the flowers to become well dried and pressed.

Using heavy mounting-board, make a mat on which the flowers are to be arranged. (White or tinted cardboard is available at stationery stores). Mark off a rectangle on the mounting board to accommodate the desired arrangement. Using a pencil and ruler, make very light lines. Place masking-tape along the outside of this line and with colored chalk, draw a heavy line along the inside of the masking tape.

Use cleansing tissue to shade the chalk from the masking tape towards the center of the rectangle. When shading is completed, remove the masking tape and spray the chalked area with fixative so that it will not smear.

WHAT ON EARTH

When the fixative is dry, arrange the flowers on the shaded chalked area in a pleasing arrangement, using open flowers, buds, and leaves to make an attractive picture. Plan the design carefully making use of the curves and colors of the dried materials.

When the final arrangement is decided upon, place a sheet of glass over the arrangement. Using a flat paste stick and ordinary library paste or white glue, slide the glass part way off the arrangement and, lifting the exposed parts of the arrangement carefully, apply paste to the undersides of the dried materials. As a part of the arrangement is pasted, cover this with the glass to hold it in place while applying paste to another part.

When completed, the arrangement may be mounted in a frame or hung on the wall, unframed.

DID YOU EVER MAKE A MOBIUS BAND?

A Mobius Band is a structure with only one surface. It is part of a study of unusual structures in a branch of science called topology.

Needed to make a Mobius Band are a pair of scissors, pencil, paste or sticking tape, and two pieces of paper, each about 10 inches long and 2 inches wide.

Lay both strips of paper on a table and mark an "A" at each end of both strips. Turn them over and mark the letter "B" on each end of that side.

Using one strip of paper, paste end "A" to end "B" making an ordinary paper band. This band will have two sides as you can prove by drawing a line down its center starting from the letter A and returning to the same spot. The other surface will have no line on it.

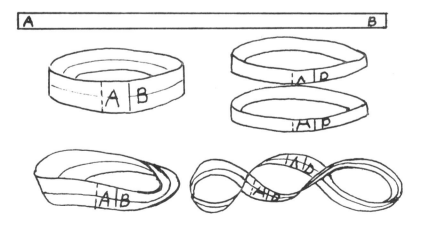

WHAT ON EARTH

Take the other strip of paper, twist it once and paste end "A" to the opposite end "A" with the "A's" touching. *This band will have only one surface which you can prove by again drawing a line down the center.* Without removing the pencil from the paper the line will go all the way along both sides of the band, proving that there is but a single surface.

Take the first band and cut it down the line you have drawn. There will be two bands each one half the width of the former band.

Cut the Mobius Band along the centerline and there will still be a single band but twice as long as before.

Now cut the first two bands down the center again. What do you get?

Do the same with the Mobius Band. What happens this time?

SEEING BACTERIA

Bacteria are very tiny, single-celled plants, so small that it takes a microscope to see a single plant, but it is possible to see groups of bacteria growing together in a colony.

Our bodies are protected by a covering of skin, as are all other living materials. As long as the skin remains whole, there is little danger of bacterial infection, but when the skin is broken, infection quickly takes place.

Let's do a few simple experiments that help us to see the damage that bacteria can do when the skin is broken.

Obtain several small glass test tubes or jars. They should have corks or tight-fitting covers.

In one tube or jar, place several small pieces of potato, apple, or squash. Cover or cork tightly and place the tube or jar in water and boil for at least fifteen minutes. Let it cool and then remove the cover and add a tiny bit of dust.

Replace the cover, wrap the tube in dark cloth or paper and set it in a warm place. At the end of three or four days, remove the wrapping and look at the contents of the test tube. Bacteria grow best where it is warm and dark. You will find a number of grey or yellow spots where the bacteria are growing on your material. Look at these with a magnifying glass or a microscope if you have one. Can you see the individual, single-celled plants? There are literally thousands of them making up each spot.

For another experiment, take two apples having skins without any holes. Puncture the skin of one apple and rub a little dust into the puncture. Rub a little dust on the skin of the second apple being careful not to puncture the skin. Wrap the apples separately in dark cloth or paper and place them in a warm spot for three or four days. Check them to see what has happened. The apple with the punctured skin should have a small infected spot showing that the apple has begun to rot where the skin was punctured. The second apple should show no damage. The dust has carried bacteria into the punctured apple, but the apple with the sound skin has not been infected.

Our own skin is like the skin of the apples. When it is damaged, bacteria gets into the puncture and infection takes place, but bacteria cannot get through whole skin. This is why we should treat punctures and cuts immediately so that infection cannot occur.

COOKING SMALL GAME

Squirrel Mulligan Stew

Skin, dress, clean, and quarter four squirrels. Place these in a pot in which a pound of lima beans has been boiling for an hour. Add a half cup of lard or shortening, 1 teaspoon salt, and 2 teaspoons ground, red pepper.

Add two cups of water and boil slowly in a covered pot until the meat falls from the bones.

Serve hot.

Rabbit Sausage

Skin and dress four or five rabbits. Wash the carcasses well in cold water and drain well. Remove all meat from the bones and cut the meat into small chunks. For each five cups of diced meat, prepare the following:

1 teaspoon salt
1 teaspoon powdered sage
½ teaspoon ground, red pepper

Mix these well and sprinkle over the meat. Stir and then grind into sausage. Shape the ground meat into patties and fry.

Roast Coon

Skin a young coon, dress and clean well in cold water. Remove all fat and parboil the coon for 1 hour in water to which 2 teaspoons of salt have been added.

Remove from the kettle, drain well, and place in a roasting pan. Add a small amount of water and roast for 2¼ hours at 375 degrees.

Roast Possum and Roast Woodchuck

Prepare and roast in the same manner as coon. While dressing woodchucks, be sure to remove the glands found under the legs.

Cooking Pheasant

Skin and wash the bird then brown for 30 minutes in frypan. Remove from pan and pressure cook at 10 lbs. pressure for 20 minutes. Remove from pressure cooker and again pan fry for 10 minutes.

Make gravy by browning 3 heaping tablespoons flour in the remaining contents of the frypan, stirring constantly. Add 1 cup water and let come to a boil while stirring. Boil for 30 seconds. Add salt and pepper to taste.

Cooking Quail and Partridge

Skin and dress birds, leaving them whole for frying. Roll in flour with a small amount of salt added. Place in frypan with hot butter or vegetable shortening and brown well on both sides. When well browned and tender, add ½ cup water, lower heat and cook slowly for 30 minutes. Gravy may be prepared as described in the above paragraph on cooking pheasant.

TANNING SMALL SKINS

The process of tanning the skins of small animals for leather-craft projects is not difficult. In addition to the actual tanning process, it is important that the skinning and curing of the hide be done carefully.

Skinning:

To make a hide of any value or usefulness, skinning must be well done.

Using a sharp knife, make cuts through the skin in the following order:

1. Slit the skin of the belly from throat to tail and up the underside of the tail as far as possible. Be sure not to puncture the body cavity.

2. Cut the skin entirely around the second joint of each leg (the elbow).

3. From the above cuts on the legs, slit the skin on the inside of the legs all the way to the belly slit and at right angles to it.

4. Slit the skin entirely around the neck.

5. Carefully peel the skin from the body, starting with the legs and tail, then the neck and body, using the sharp knife as little as possible and taking care not to cut through the skin.

Curing or Drying:

Tack the skin to a wall or wooden frame, keeping its original size and shape and placing small tacks or nails at the extreme margins where the holes will not damage the skin. Keep the flesh side on the outside.

Dry in the open air in a shady place. Avoid heat and freezing as these may cause the skin to crack.

To preserve the skin, rub salt into the flesh side of the skin as soon as it has been stretched and tacked on the drying frame, and again after a day or two of drying.

WHAT ON EARTH

To make a good hide, all tissue and fatty particles must be removed before the skin is entirely dry. A blunt-edged knife or putty knife make good tools to use as scrapers. Place the skin on a firm surface and scrape towards yourself using pressure with the blunt edge of the tool on the skin to remove the tissue and fat.

When the skin is entirely dry, store it in a cool, dry place until you are ready to tan it.

(A fresh skin attracts blowflies which will lay their eggs on the skin especially in warm weather. Their egg masses look like fine yellow sawdust. Use wire screening if necessary to keep them from the skin while it is drying.)

Acid Tanning:

This method is fast, requiring from 15 to 48 hours depending upon the strength of the acid used. It may be used either on a pelt or on a skin from which the hair has been removed. (See page 150 for directions for dehairing a skin.)

Prepare one of the following solutions in a quantity to cover the skins to be tanned, increasing the proportion of ingredients as needed to make increased amounts of the solutions.

Solution #1: (15 to 24 hours required for tanning)
2 quarts of distilled water or rainwater
1 ounce alum
1 pint table salt
½ ounce chemically pure sulphuric acid

Solution #2: (24 to 48 hours required for tanning)
4 quarts distilled water or rainwater
1 pint table salt
2 ounces oxalic acid

CAUTION is necessary when using acid. Wear rubber gloves. Use wooden or glazed earthenware containers. First dissolve the dry ingredients, then add the acid slowly to the solution. If any acid is spilled or touches the skin, flush the area with water *immediately* and then neutralize the acid with a solution of baking soda.

The Tanning Process:

Using either one of the above solutions, immerse the pelt, covering it completely with the solution. If the skin is dry, soak it thoroughly in water before placing it in the solution.

If solution #1 is used, the alum acts as an astringent and shrinks the skin. After 5 to 6 hours in this solution, the skin should be removed and stretched back to the original size and shape. Wearing rubber gloves, strip the solution from the skin by sliding one hand down the skin while holding it with the other. Stretch until smooth, place it again in the solution and leave for an additional 12 to 15 hours. At the end of this time, remove the skin from the solution, strip out the excess liquid and rinse it well in plenty of clear water.

Some acid will remain in the skin. This acid should be neutralized by covering the skin for 3 to 4 hours with a solution of 1½ cups washing soda in one gallon of water. Rinse completely in clear water and hang the skin up until nearly dry.

While the skin is still slightly damp, start the process of *breaking in* the skin, stretching, kneading, and rubbing the skin with the fingers until it is dry and soft. Drawing the skin back and forth across the edge of a board or table may help the softening process.

When the skin is soft and dry, rub the flesh side with neat's-foot oil or a good cooking oil until the entire flesh side is well covered with the oil.

Let the oiled skin stand for one-half hour, then rub it with a dry, absorbent cloth to remove any excess oil. Remove any oil that may have touched the fur side.

Wash the skin with warm water and mild soap flakes. Rinse well in clean water, stretch to its original size, shape, and hang it up to dry.

Dehairing Small Skins:

If you wish the finished product to be without hair, use one of the following methods of dehairing. Always soak the skin in water before placing it in a dehairing solution. Dehairing must be done before tanning.

Using Wood Ashes

Use only the white ashes left from a wood fire. Mix this with water to form a thin paste. Cover the hair side of the skin with this paste allowing it to stand until the hair loosens. This may take anywhere from four to twelve hours depending on the type and condition of the skin. Remove the paste as soon as the hair loosens and can be removed by scraping. Some of the paste can be scraped off and the remainder washed from the skin.

Using Lime Water Solution

Prepare a lime water solution by mixing two pounds of unslaked lime in one gallon of water. Add the lime slowly while stirring carefully. Do not allow the solution to spill or splash on hands or clothing. If it does, wash it off immediately with plenty of water.

Place the wet skin in the lime water solution. After one hour, test to see if the hair is loose. Wear rubber gloves and handle the skin with a stick. When the hair is loosened, remove the skin from the solution, rinsing it several times in clean water.

Removing the Hair:

Using either of the above methods, when the hair is loosened, remove it by scraping.

Holding the skin taut across a small board, scrape with a putty knife or other blunt-edged tool until all of the hair has been removed.

The skin will still be covered by a thin layer called the scarf skin. A suede finish may be obtained by removing this scarf skin through continued scraping, or the skin may be left with the scarf skin intact.

Tanning should follow immediately, but if this is not possible, the skin may be left in clear water for several hours until the tanning can be done.

Tanning the Dehaired Skin:

Either of the acid methods of tanning may be used as described previously, or one of the following simpler methods may be used.

Kerosene and Soapsuds Method of Tanning —

Using one bar laundry soap to one gallon of water, shave the soap into the water, stirring until all of the soap has dissolved. Allow the solution to clear, then stir in kerosene, using as much as will form an emulsion which does not separate when allowed to stand. This will involve a little experimentation.

Place the dehaired skin in this solution and soak for four days. Hang the skin on a line allowing it to dry until it is only slightly damp. While still slightly damp, "break-in" or soften the skin as described below. This is most important if a good tanned skin is desired.

Salt and Alum Method —

Prepare a saturated solution using two parts of salt and one part of alum. Two cups salt and one cup alum in one gallon of hot water will provide enough saturated solution for a large skin. There should be enough solution to cover the skin completely. A saturated solution is one that has dissolved all of the materials it can hold. To make sure that saturation is complete, a little of the alum and salt mixture should remain in the bottom of the mixing container.

WHAT ON EARTH

Cool and strain the solution, pour it over the skin and allow it to soak for three days. Remove the skin from the solution, hang it over a line to drip until nearly dry when it will be ready for the *breaking in* process.

Breaking In (Softening) a Skin:

Skins tanned by any of the above methods must be broken in or softened before they are entirely dry. *Breaking in* a skin is the process of rubbing and stretching the skin before it dries out. This will change the skin from a tough, harsh rawhide to a soft, pliable leather. In softening the skin, care must be taken not to split or break it.

Small skins may be softened by rubbing by hand. Larger skins are pulled across the edge of a board or a rounded metal edge, changing the skin from side to side and from surface to surface, and continuing until all stiffness has disappeared and the leather is soft, pliable, and uniform in color. The skin is now ready for use and may be stored until needed.

Waterproofing Skins:

To make skins water resistant, apply warm neat's-foot oil to all parts of the skin before breaking in or softening is done. Allow the oil to remain overnight until the oil has penetrated the skin.

Stretch the skin to its original size and shape and nail on a flat surface to partially dry. While stretching the skin, wash off any remaining oil with a warm, mild soap solution, then break-in or soften it as described previously.

BIBLIOGRAPHY

SELECTED BIBLIOGRAPHY

The following list of publications, to the best knowledge of the author, provides the most useful references available for the type of material included in this book.

BOOKS

Abbott, Robert T., *Introducing Seashells,* Van Nostrand, New York, New York, 1955.

Bale, R. O., *Stepping Stones to Nature,* Burgess Publishing Co., Minneapolis, Minnesota, 1960.

Bale, R. O., *Creative Nature Crafts,* Burgess Publishing Co., Minneapolis, Minnesota, 1959.

Bale, R. O., *Outdoor Living,* Burgess Publishing Co., Minneapolis, Minnesota, 1961.

Bean, L. L., *Hunting, Fishing and Camping,* Freeport, Maine.

Carhart, A. H., *Fishing is Fun,* MacMillan, New York, N.Y., 1950.

Carrington, Richard, *Story of Our Earth,* Harper and Brothers, New York, New York, 1956.

Cassell, Sylvia, *Nature Games and Activities,* Harper & Brothers, New York, New York, 1956.

Cavanna, Betty, *First Book of Sea Shells,* Watts, New York, New York, 1955.

Colby, C. B., *First Fish,* Coward-McCann, New York, New York, 1953.

Garnow, George, *Biography of the Earth,* Viking, 1941.

Hammett, Cartherine T., and Carol M. Horrocks, *Creative Crafts for Campers,* New York, New York, 1957.

Jaeger, Ellsworth, *Nature Crafts,* Macmillan Co., New York, New York, 1950.

Jaeger, Ellsworth, *Wildwood Wisdom,* The Mac Millian Co., New York, New York, 1950.

Mason, Bernard S., *Woodcraft,* A. S. Barnes and Co., New York, New York, 1939.

McClane, A. J., *Wise Fisherman's Encyclopedia,* Wise, New York, New York, 1951.

Moore, R. E., *The Earth We Live On,* Knopf, New York, New York, 1956.

Rodman, O. H. P., *Boy's Complete Book of Fresh and Salt Water Fishing,* Little, 1947.

Rutstrum, Calvin, *New Way of Wilderness,* Mac Millan Co., New York, New York, 1959.

Schnieder, Herman and Nina, *Rocks, Rivers and the Changing Earth,* W. R. Scott, New York, New York, 1952.

Seton, E. T., *The Birchbark Roll of Woodcraft,* A. S. Barnes and Co., New York, New York, o.p.

Seton, E. T., *Book of Woodcraft,* Doubleday, Page and Co., 1922.

Walton, Izaak, *Compleat Angler,* Modern Library.

Welch, Fay, *When You are in the Woods,* State University College of Forestry, Syracuse, New York, 1950.

Wells, H. G. *Outline of History,* Garden City Books, Garden City, L. I., New York, 1949.

Zim, Herbert S. and Hobart M. Smith, *Reptiles and Amphibians,* Simon and Schuster, New York, New York, 1956.

Zim, Herbert S., *What's Inside the Earth,* Morrow, New York, New York, 1953.

PERIODICALS AND PAMPHLETS

"Campfires and Camp Cookery" — Cornell Rural School Leaflet, Vol. 17, No. 2, November 1923, Cornell University, Ithaca, N. Y. (Out of print)

"4-H Club Insect Manual" Miscellaneous Publication No. 318, United States Department of Agriculture, Washington D. C., 1939.

"Conservation and Nature Activities" Audubon Society of Canada, 177 Jarvis St., Toronto, Canada, 1951.

"Meals and Nights in the Open" (mimeographed) by J. A. Cope and Fred E. Winch Jr., Department of Conservation, Cornell University, Ithaca, N.Y. — Revised June 1951.

"Little Climates" Cornell Rural School Leaflet, Vol. 37, No. 3, January 1944, Cornell University, Ithaca, New York.

"Common Poisonous Plants" by W. C. Muenscher and W. T. Winne, Cornell Extension Bulletin 538, Sept. 1942, Cornell University, Ithaca, New York.

"Nature Activities for Summer Camps" National Audubon Society, 1130 Fifth Ave., New York, New York, 1950.

"Weeds of the Northeast" C. E. Phillips, University of Delaware, Agricultural Field Manual No. 1, Experiment Station, Newark, Delaware.

The Sport of Orienteering, Silva, Inc., Laporte, Indiana.

INDEX

INDEX

INDEX

A knowledge of the earth; its land masses and its seas; its plant and animal life; its many climates; its rocks and minerals; its natural resources; how each is affected by the others; and finally where mankind fits into it all, helps determine how each of us shall live.

6382